PONY

ELOISE SNAPE

CURRENCY PRESS
The performing arts publisher

GRIFFIN
THEATRE
COMPANY

CURRENT THEATRE SERIES

First published in 2023
by Currency Press Pty Ltd,
PO Box 2287, Strawberry Hills, NSW, 2012, Australia
enquiries@currency.com.au
www.currency.com.au

in association with Griffin Theatre Company

Typeset by Brighton Gray for Currency Press.
Printed by Fineline Print + Copy Services, Revesby, NSW.
Cover features Briallen Clarke, photo by Brett Boardman, design by Alphabet.

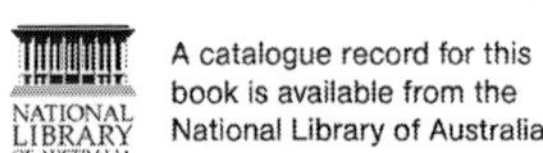

Contents

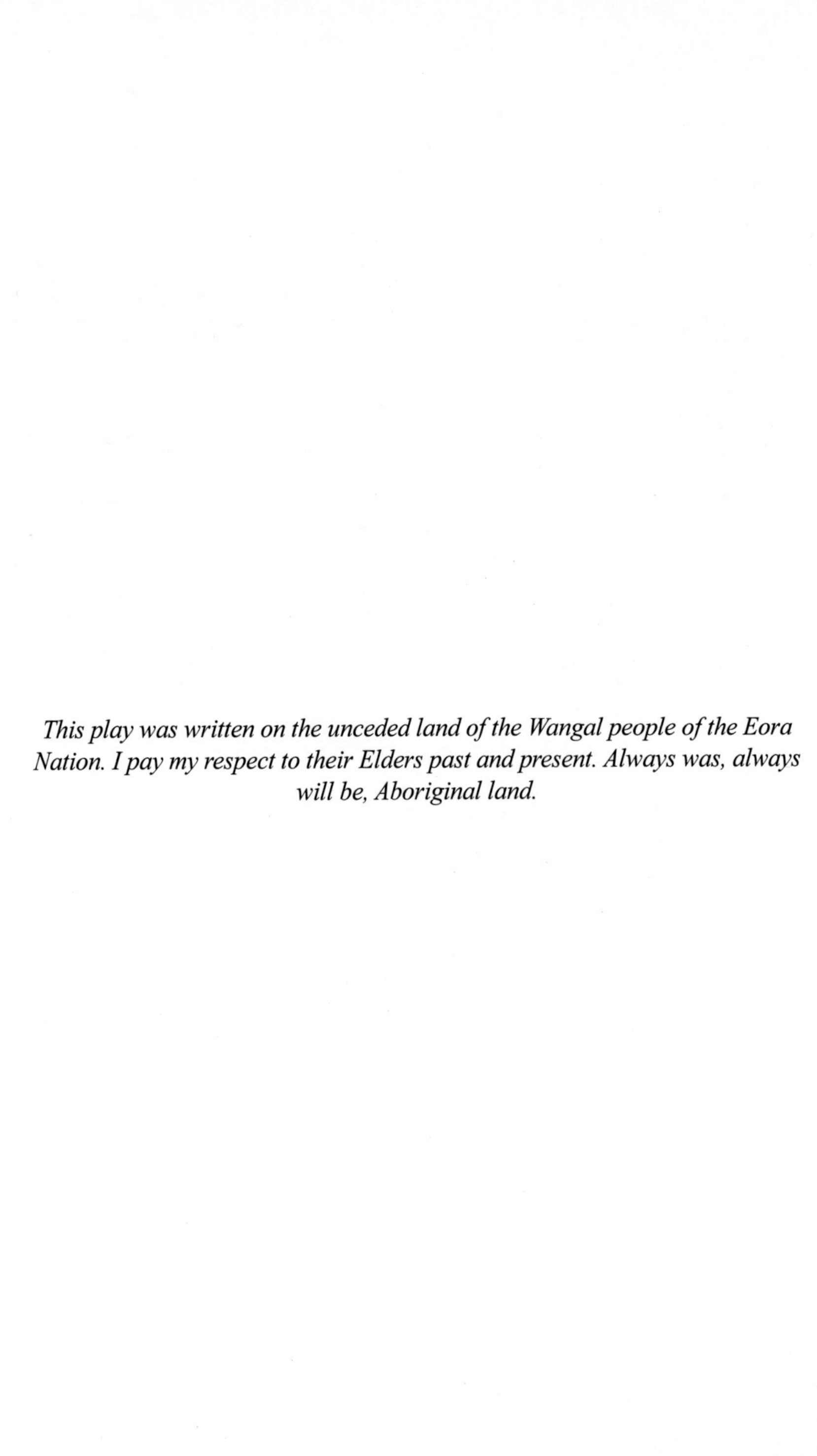

This play was written on the unceded land of the Wangal people of the Eora Nation. I pay my respect to their Elders past and present. Always was, always will be, Aboriginal land.

Pony was first produced by Griffin Theatre Company at the SBW Stables Theatre, Gadigal country, Sydney, on 12 May 2023, with the following cast:

HAZEL	Briallen Clarke

Director and Dramaturg, Anthea Williams
Production Designer, Isabel Hudson
Lighting Designer, Verity Hampson
Composer and Sound Designer, Me-Lee Hay
Stage Manager, Jen Jackson

CHARACTERS

All to be played by the same actor.

HAZEL

MRS TWINKLES/JANICE, Rhyme Time host

LIV, Hazel's best friend from university

REON, Liv's son

PATRICK, Hazel's partner

BROTHER-IN-LAW, Patrick's brother

CLEMENTINE, Hazel's mum

ESME, Hazel's nana

HARRY, Hazel's on/off again ex

HAZEL'S COUSIN

GEN, Hazel's schoolfriend

MEL, Gen's partner

HAZEL'S AUNT

PUPPET-MURDERING TODDLER, Rhyme Time regular

GINGER-HAIRED TODDLER, Rhyme Time regular

ROD STEWART BABY, Rhyme Time regular

HOT DAD, Rhyme Time regular

RAELENE, Rhyme Time regular

BIG MUSCLE PARTY HOST

MAJOR VINCENT, a stripper from Canberra

SHORT MAN WEARING TURTLENECK, a one-night stand

RPA. NURSE

TRISH, a midwife/teenage male gymnastics coach

FIVE COUPLES, at Relax Birth Course

DEADBEAT DAD, at Relax Birth Course

TRACEY, Liv's mum

WOMAN AT TABLE, dining at fancy restaurant

WAITRESS WITH SLEEVE TATTOO, working at fancy restaurant

WOMAN IN KAFTAN

STRIPPER COP 1

STRIPPER COP 2

TIM THE ANAESTHETIST

This play text went to press before the end of rehearsals and may differ from the play as performed.

MRS TWINKLES: [*spoken*] Hello everyone. Hello everyone. How are you today?

Hello everyone. Hello everyone. How are you today?

HAZEL: Mrs Twinkles delivers this weeks 'Hello' song directly to me. It's been a month, and she's welcomed me back. She looks at me warmly. I take a deep breath. I remove my jacket.

Her pink bob moves with extra buoyancy this morning.

I wonder what kind of shampoo she uses. Is she a L'Oréal kind of woman? Salon Selectives (is that even a thing anymore)? Expensive I-got-done-up-the backside-by-my-hairdresser brand and like a trip to Aldi walked out with seven different types of hair product and an air-conditioning unit when all I came for was a blow-dry. Or is she one these types who swears by the 'I don't wash my hair and it just gets cleaner' method of haircare which, let's be honest, is not a thing. I'm just too afraid to tell you that you smell like an old shoe.

I would encourage the actor to improvise or play with the audience in this first section, if it feels right.

No. Mrs Twinkles is a woman of integrity.

MRS TWINKLES: Hello everyone. Hello everyone. How are you to—

HAZEL: I join in, sheepishly. Sans jacket.

It's been one month. And after an eventful hiatus, I feel relief. I feel, free.

But the songs at Glebe Library Rhyme Time still have to be spoken. Pandemic rules apply.

Glebe Library Rhyme Time is no joke. It is a sacred space, where twice a week, exhausted parents rely on Mrs Twinkles to entertain their tiny demons for a solid gold half an hour. They congregate on the musty blue carpet in the back room of the library and Mrs Twinkles sings like she's auditioning for *Australian Idol* to the smell of breast milk and baby shit. It's a highly competitive position too. Mrs Twinkles knows one wrong move and there is a queue of library employees waiting to step up to the plate and prove that they should have been cast as Eliza Doolittle in the Willoughby Musical Society's production of *My Fair Lady*, all those years ago.

But since Covid, the library continues to take a military approach to the rules, and here we are. Still. Speak-singing.

It's like being at a university spoken-word poetry night. Some songs translate to speech much more effectively than others. 'Incy Wincy Spider' becomes quite profound. 'Twinkle Twinkle Little Star' has dark shades of nihilism. 'The Wheels On the Bus' is, well …

[*Spoken*] The wheels on the bus go round and round. Round and round. Round and round. The wheels on the bus go round and round.

All.

Day.

Long.

The lady with the perfect ginger-haired baby boy is doing a horrible job of pretending she's looking at something behind me. There's Raelene with the oversized lips, right up the front with her strange-looking two-year-old who keeps ripping the felt puppets out of Mrs Twinkles' hands, whispering in his mother's ear and pointing his fat little finger in my direction. Raelene looks at me awkwardly. They all look at me awkwardly.

Round and round.

Round and round.

A baby with a head of hair resembling Rod Stewart circa 1976 crawls towards me.

I smile at her.

She starts crying.

Round and round. Round and round.

Breathe Hazel. Breathe.

Don't take it personally. After the, the … 'incident'—no baby with any boundaries is going to come near you.

The old wooden library door creaks open and Hot Dad peeks through. Hot Dad is all broad shoulders, biceps and baby-carrying hands. Hot Dad and his daughter shuffle discreetly to a cushion on the floor, trying to avoid the disapproving gaze of Mrs Twinkles who is now halfway through *That's Not My Kitten*.

That's Not My Kitten is a Rhyme Time classic. It's one in a series of That's Not My books. *That's Not My Unicorn*. *That's Not My Bunny*. *That's Not My Otter*.

MRS TWINKLES: That's not my kitten. Its paws are too smooth. That's not my kitten. Its tummy is too furry.

HAZEL: My husband's brother developed his own filthy version: *That's Not My Wife*.

BROTHER-IN-LAW: That's not my wife. Her titties are too saggy. That's not my wife. Her pussy is too loose.

If it feels right, the actor is welcome to acknowledge someone directly in the audience with a 'too much?'

HAZEL: If Liv was here we'd be thinking the same thing.

Liv is my best friend.

Liv, in fact, introduced me to Glebe Library Rhyme Time. Liv was a nervous wreck about anything that involved being amongst babies, despite just having had one, so I promised I would go with her to her first one.

She is back in the past.

The night before, however, we had been at my cousin's hens' party.

My cousin is six years older and the kind of person you desperately wished was your big sister, when you were on the precipice of puberty. However, when you hit your early twenties and she passed you her rum and Coke and slurred: 'You better have this or I won't know who's pounding my arse later,' you are thankful to the genie that you did not get your wish.

So it was no surprise that for *her* hens' party we ended up at Sydney's hottest male-strip revue: Bankstown Sports Club's Big Muscle Party.

It was everything you would have hoped for at a sophisticated hens:

Frozen margaritas spilling over the top of feather boas.

High-pitched squeals intense enough to send the local domestic pets on heat.

My infamous auntie in her mesh singlet flirting with the security guard.

The occasional distant sounds of 'more chilli' coming from the pokie room.

All while sweaty oversized torsos gyrate in a decidedly family-friendly manner to … dun dun dun … Ginuwine's 'Pony'.

Esme, my nana, my soulmate, the life of every party, was so determined to come that she insisted Clementine must be there to 'help her up and down the stairs'. Conveniently and much to Clementine's frustration, there were zero stairs to contend with. Nana hoots—a penis balloon tied to the top of her four-pronged cane.

As the platoon of steroid-induced men trot off the stage in a sea of sticky feathers and stripper dollars, a thin pimply teenager starts wiping our table with a sad, crusty, Chux wipe. Clementine sees this as her chance at distraction and awkwardly and unsuccessfully tries to start a conversation with him about his working hours and how he manages to stay on top of his schoolwork.

I glare at her to stop being such a killjoy. She ignores me and keeps being a killjoy and we take the Chux as our cue to move the party on.

Then an announcement blasts over the cheap crackling speakers. The microphone blows out and Nana's hearing aid screeches. She doesn't notice.

BIG MUSCLE PARTY HOST: Hey hey hey team we have a surprise for one of our lucky ladies out there—a private trip to Muscle Town and back with Major Vincent! Hazel. We are looking for a Hazel—

HAZEL: Before he has time to publicly announce my full name, Nana, who is now beside herself with glee and is waving that four-penis'd cane with full force in my direction, starts yelling:

ESME: She's there! Hazel's right there!

HAZEL: Nana winks at me and there's no time to even pick up my penis straw before Liv has grabbed my wrist as we are dragged down a corridor of horror-film-esque doors. With my other hand I try and grab Gen, who's holding on to Mel, her girlfriend, and use them as shields. Gen breaks free, throwing her hand up in my face:

GEN: No. Please. No more balls. I haven't seen this many balls since I was sixteen.

HAZEL: Next thing I know I am being dragged into a small dark room the size of a linen cupboard. Liv holds my hand and squeals with delight.

The two of us sit in silence as we wait for Major Vincent.

Silence.

I wonder if he oils his cra—?

The door swings open and a huge square-shaped beast of a man enters the room wearing a plush pink robe. His skin is glistening with what I can only assume is vegetable oil? If this was *Masterchef*, he was ready to be thrown onto a hibachi.

MAJOR VINCENT: [*in an unusually high-pitched voice*] So, um, which one of you ladies is Hazel?

HAZEL: [*to audience*] Oof. Voice not matching visuals. Abort mission.

I nod.

Major Vincent looks at his watch and without a word mounts Liv.

LIV: Oh … thank you.

HAZEL: Thank you?

He begins thrusting and grinding. To silence.

Silence.

I turn and look at Liv. This is her first proper night out since having a baby. Her face fluctuates between confusion, joy and exhaustion. The more she tries not to laugh, the more intense our muffled giggles become and all is right in the world.

HAZEL: Um, no music?

I quickly pull my phone out of my pocket, open Spotify and hit play on my Bad Bitches playlist.

Major Vincent frowns at me.

MAJOR VINCENT: Shhh.

HAZEL: I turn it off.

He begins to derobe. In silence.

Silence.

The actor can improvise the sound here. Anything that feels right, and a bit off.

Yeeeeah!

I let out a sound that feels right for the situation but it clearly isn't.

Liv, through stifled gasps, she starts a slow clap.

In time to Major Vincent's thrusts.

I join in.

It's hard to keep in time as his humping is all over the shop.

I'm beginning to realise why there is no soundtrack.

Suddenly he leap frogs across onto me. It's not as smooth as I would have expected from a professional. He places both of my hands firmly on each buttock cheek, checks his watch again and continues to grind robotically.

Liv and I keep clapping, now quite aggressively, until it all becomes too much and I say:

So Major Vincent, where are you from?

MAJOR VINCENT: [*surprised*] Canberra?

HAZEL: … Our nation's capital! Yeah. Great. Um, when did you move to Sydney? Was it for work? To, um, get away from all the politicians and the sex shops?

MAJOR VINCENT: —

HAZEL: Sorry, but … I have to fill the silence. This is so awkward.

MAJOR VINCENT: It's about to get a whole lot more awkward when—

HAZEL: Major Vincent takes no prisoners. All I can see is the blur of a sparkling golden G-string and two mishapen oily testicles toppling out the sides and gliding towards my face. It's terrifying.

As his balls flap back and forth like a giant pendulum, he starts to answer my questions more sincerely and once he starts speaking? He does not stop.

Within five minutes we had learnt about his decision to move from Canberra to Sydney to escape a traumatic relationship. And that the work for male strippers had become challenging. He spoke about the weather in Canberra and that the cold was affecting his mental health and his … career. A small tear rolled down his cheek. Liv offers him a tissue and gives him advice about a mental-health care plan.

As we stand outside Bankstown Sports Centre, Clementine and Nana's Uber finally pulls up.

ESME: Brilliant show. Great story. Solid cast.

HAZEL: She slaps me on the arse and toddles off to the Prius, the now-deflated penis balloon limp on top of her cane.

Even Clementine laughs:

CLEMENTINE: Oh thank goodness. I didn't think I'd ever be able to get her to come home.

HAZEL: I wave them off and turn to Liv. Now they've gone, we can finally let our hair down.

LIV: I need to go. I'm dead. I've died inside.

HAZEL: No no no. You can't. Please Liv. I can't do my auntie solo. She's already flashed one tit. And the other one is covered in such a thin layer of mesh, I don't know if I can save the party from it.

LIV: Hazel, your auntie's tits aren't the problem here.

HAZEL: I look down at Liv's shirt and the two perfect breast-sized milk circles that have taken over.

Silence.

Hey Liv.

LIV: Don't. Don't say it.

HAZEL: Remember the Oak Milk factory we used to stop at on the way to Splendour?

LIV: I can't, okay Hazel?

HAZEL: Liv leaves. I thought she'd be busting for a night out. We were only just getting started. She's just got to get that baby on to bottles, stat.

The next morning, as I mentioned before, is Liv's first ever Glebe Library Rhyme Time and because I am such a good friend, it is also my first ever Glebe Library Rhyme Time. I even bring her a coffee.

LIV: Hazel, really?

HAZEL: I look at Liv quizzically.

I touch my face.

I look down.

Blood?

Oh.

Images start flooding my brain hole.

My cousin and her buck tied up in leather.

Playing 'pin the dick on the hot man' poster.

Pinning real dicks.

Touching random dicks.

Rain?

Wrestling in the herb garden.

Someone crying over their dead mint.

My auntie's tits.

Both of them.

Me in a mesh singlet? Who has a permanent marker?

My broken car window.

Side-swiping a dick as I vomit into a curb.

Vomiting into a bucket.

Vomiting into a toilet.

A damp, hairy, chest slowly sliding along my cheek.

Waking up next to … my ex, Harry.

Fuck.

I'm okay. Don't worry. It's just a few cuts. You think they have a first-aid, thing. Ugh.

LIV: What?

HAZEL: I fucked Harry.

Silence.

Did you hear me? Harry! Harry Harry. Chode Harry. Harry. Harry with chode.

LIV: Your face.

HAZEL: I pull out my phone and look into the camera. My face has been transformed into a giant vagina. My nose is a clitoris and my mouth has been used to form the vaginal lips. On my forehead is written 'insert dick here'. It's quite impressive.

Fucking hell!

LIV: Hazel, this is a library. Just … rein it in.

HAZEL: [*whispering*] Fucking hell!

Liv is mortified. Old Liv would have laughed.

New Liv wets herself if she laughs.

The first time I was privy to one of her post-partum urine emergencies was when I took her along to a circuit-training class. I would get two weeks free off my membership for bringing along a friend and her whining about her lack of motivation was becoming a bit of a bore. Unfortunately the star-jumps were too extreme and after her tenth a large patch of liquid formed over her crutch area.

Poor Liv. It's the worst feeling, I know. I remember when I was little, often having those dreams where you sit on the toilet doing a big, juicy wee and then of course you wake and find you literally are doing a wee. Dad would always come in and change the sheets.

Sometimes he would try to distract me with a midnight concert on his funny little ukulele.

Silence.

Eventually I couldn't put up with Liv wetting herself in public anymore, so, being the excellent friend that I am, I came up with the best birthday present ever. Do I buy her a lifetime supply of Tena Lady pads? No. I buy her the gift of confidence.

I surprised Liv and her five-month post-partum pelvic floor with a Killing Kittens sex workshop—'A bag of tools for his tool. How to give him a mind-blowing O'. The workshop was run by a sex-fluencer whose Instagram selfies were enviable, but in person it became apparent five minutes into the workshop that her face didn't move.

In front of us in her Bondi dance hall, are ten platforms reminiscent of the pummel horses I used to desperately avoid in primary-school gym class. Hanging from the ceiling are ropes and swings.

Liv and I giggle our way through an afternoon of sexy tricks and techniques that feel like an audition for Cirque du Soleil. Liv looks a little pale but says she needs a drink. We leave confident and ready to apply our learning.

An hour later we sip negronis at a small bar in a backstreet of Surry Hills. A short man wearing a turtleneck approaches us.

SHORT MAN WEARING TURTLENECK: It's … Harriet, isn't it?

HAZEL: It turns out he recognised me from radio lab, which was one of my third-year classes at uni. We had to record and produce our own radio docos.

SHORT MAN WEARING TURTLENECK: You did the research assignment on—

HAZEL: Reality TV contestants and mental health.

SHORT MAN WEARING TURTLENECK: Ha.

HAZEL: Liv jumps in, right on cue.

LIV: And I think if I recall correctly, yours was on vaccinations and autism?

SHORT MAN WEARING TURTLENECK: Sorry, you are?

LIV: Olivia Grace. I—

SHORT MAN WEARING TURTLENECK: *The* Olivia Grace! Yes yes yes. I remember you. You bailed from completing your major work on Marion Mahony Griffin. Such a shame. You had real potential.

LIV: I know. I became an architect. An under-acknowledged one—

HAZEL: Much like our capital's *real* designer Marion Mahony Griffin.

I didn't mind that he was a misogynist who thought my name was Harriet. I was ready to test out the 'rotating porpoise' and he looked game.

I'm now mid aerial twist and Turtleneck is beside himself.

SHORT MAN WEARING TURTLENECK: [*sounds of pleasure that are actually pain*] Oh, oh, ah, oh, ahhhhhhhh, oh ah ah ah ah ah AH AH OH OH OW OW—

HAZEL: Crunch.

He curls up into a ball and rocks in the foetal position.

I see blood.

I've killed Turtleneck's dick.

At RPA, I sit by his hospital bed until his sister arrives. The nurse on duty gives me a nod of sympathy. When I return home, I find his turtleneck and mop up his dick blood.

If it feels right, the actor is welcome to acknowledge the audience here with a 'yep, feeling a little off sir?'

I guess that's what you get for being an anti-vaxxer. I never hear from him again.

Take two. I decide that clearly the problem was all him and that I am actually a master of the porpoise. I just need to try again.

Not long after she's finished her maternity leave, Liv invites me to a work function. Her firm are putting on a 'do' to launch a big project. I don't care what it's for, I am there for three reasons:

To support my best friend

To make it up to her for sleeping with a possible flat-earther?

The very corporate cheese platter.

The positioning of the various wheels is architecturally very pleasing and the ratio of cheese versus biscuit versus quince is perfect.

As I'm floating around the brie, a dark-haired man with broken glasses leans across to cut a slice. As he pulls the knife out he brings the whole wheel with him and it falls to the floor with a thud. He bends over to pick up the now-floor cheese and his lens falls out and sticks to the brie. He looks up at me with a mix of apology, embarrassment and delight:

PATRICK: Did you hear about the cheese factory that exploded in France?

HAZEL: Um, no.

PATRICK: All that was left was debris.

HAZEL: I have found rotating porpoise take two.

We have mind-blowing sex. I come first. Now is the time.

I flip. I spin. I twist. I am powerful. I am sex goddess of the world.

He is coming.

PATRICK: [*sounds of pleasure that are actually pain*] Uh, uh, um, Hazel, Hazel, um uh, ow, oh, wow, oh, wow, oh, okay ow, ow, no please stop—

HAZEL: I kill his dick.

I am now the killer of not one, but two dicks. Killing Kittens takes on a whole new meaning for me.

At RPA, I sit by his hospital bed until his brother arrives.

The same nurse is on duty. She nods her head again.

As I'm mopping up dick blood and feeling like Bill Murray in *Groundhog Day* I think, well that's a shame. That guy was cool.

Pause.

Two-and-a-half years later, Nana is walking me down the aisle, into the arms of that cool guy. Patrick. His name is Patrick. As we take the first steps out of the bridal villa, I begin to panic. She squeezes my hand and says:

ESME: If you break a man's penis with the rotating porpoise and he still comes back for more, you know he is a keeper.

HAZEL: When Patrick sees me for the first time, his eyes well and I think: I don't think anyone has ever loved me as much as this.

I look over to Clementine. I can't work out if she is full of joy or her heart is breaking. I smile at Patrick's dad. And for just a moment, I feel overwhelmingly sad.

She is back in the present.

PUPPET MURDERER: Mummy her breath smells—

HAZEL: Back in Glebe Library Rhyme Time, I look down at my phone and there is a text from Liv. 'Coffee in ten?' Round and round. Round and round.

I hope it's just Liv today. I don't have it in me. I have tried. I have tried so hard to get along with Reon.

You know those people who look at the world like it's out to get them? He is constantly on the defense. And judgemental. I'm actually convinced he's a narcissist. It's all about him. Liv does everything. The meals. The cleaning. He's controlling. He won't let her go anywhere without him. Old Liv would never have put up with his shit.

I guess when your name is a spelling mistake you're going to have some issues. I thought it was funny at first, a little joke between Reon and I. I'd call him Leon. I'd call him Deon. Anything but his shit name.

It was after his second birthday party that Liv finally cracked it at me.

I had offered to babysit that evening so she and Justin could have a date night to celebrate surviving those first two bullshit years. Unfortunately things went downhill when the smell of burning turd started to permeate their house. Reon had done a poo in the bath, cleverly stuffed all the pieces into a scented candle and used my lighter to light it. I was genuinely impressed.

When Liv got home the only thing she could say was:

LIV: Please just call him Reon.

HAZEL: Agh.

She feels a kick.

Okay, okay. Today I will call him Reon. Only six months until he starts school.

She is back in the past.

One year after the wedding, my libido had been demolished by my Mirena, and I was completely over every awful choice of contraception that only seemed to work because I wasn't interested in having my lady parts touched anymore. And I wasn't worried when I finally decided to have my IUD taken out. I mean, it had taken years of IVF for Liv to get pregnant. Sure, her endo was being a bitch. But what are the chances of actually falling pregnant?

Plus we'd done so much rooting on our Italian yacht *Below Deck*-vibes honeymoon, I was happy for the rest.

For those playing at home, *Below Deck* is a reality-television show, which chronicles the lives of the crew working onboard a super yacht during charter season, in various exotic destinations. The show is the perfect mix of travel, drama and hot people. It's also mildly educational in its exploration of life 'below deck'.

Each night Patrick and I went to bed, I would hide my phone under the covers and watch, with my headphones in, until it would send me into a blissful sleep. I would dream about Captain Sandy accusing me for having a problem with authority, panic every time we have to drop anchor in tricky but delightful ports of the Med and party hard with Chief Stew Hannah and her crew in Croatia.

This one particular night, I crawled in next to Patrick, rolled over, discreetly put the covers over my head and loaded up the next ep when:

PATRICK: What are you doing?

What's under the cover?

Hazel, are you watching porn? It's okay if you are, just don't lie to me. You don't have to hide it.

I don't mind. We could watch together—

HAZEL: It's really not porn it's—

When Patrick figures out I'm so addicted to *Below Deck* that I can't fall asleep without it, we go from what is a mild debate about the hideous nature of reality television, to screens in the bedroom, to don't try to control me, to I'm not—I'm just suggesting it's not good for you, to you're trying to run my life, to we're married shouldn't we come to an agreement about these things and what's good for our sleep, to doors slamming in the night, Nana getting a distraught call at one a.m., running up the street threatening to leave forever, returning five minutes later, a tearful reunion and then passionate, angry, romantic and ultimately for the purposes of this story, *unprotected* make-up sex.

The next morning Patrick rolls over and spoons me.

PATRICK: Well that was … Are you okay?

HAZEL: I'm fine.

I wasn't fine. I wasn't ready. I mean, I was ready. I was thirty-seven. And highly aware that since I turned thirty-five I have been considered geriatric, in pregnancy terms. At my last pap smear, my doctor didn't hold back in letting me know my eggs were dying fast. Round and round. Round and round.

After Patrick leaves for work that morning, I pull on a pair of ill-fitting overalls and cover them with an oversized jacket, desperately trying to conceal any evidence of baby-brewing. It's February in Sydney but I was dressed for Arctic temps, power-walking towards the bus stop in an attempt to not be that guy who is late for work, but is definitely late for work and still managed to get a coffee and bacon and egg roll on the way.

On a side note, I never dreamt of working in community radio but I like the people and more importantly, the desk and brain space it gives me to work on my *Survivor* application. Clementine describes this job as a 'stepping stone to greater things', but as we all know, the Golden Age of Radio was the 1920s so I'm what? About a hundred years late for the yacht. Sorry, *Below Deck* reference. Clementine on the other hand, was the first woman to receive the Vincent's fellowship from Sydney University Med School so …

I made it to the bus stop. But then I turned back around. And walked. And walked. Faster. And faster. I didn't know where I was going but it was like I had to move the sperm out of me. Around me. Off me? I didn't know which but as I passed the library I heard music. Nursery rhymes. I felt compelled to stop and without thought, began following the sea of prams into that musty old council library room. I crept in and stood at the back. It was the same Rhyme Time I went to with Liv—almost four years before. I watched the parents and their babies smiling and giggling. Mrs Twinkles appeared in all her seemingly ageless glory. Everyone began singing. The songs felt familiar. I felt …

No-one knows I come here every week. Not even Liv.

Finally, after some random bleeding I sat on the toilet and peed on ten different sticks. It was by the tenth that I finally realised I needed to call Nana.

ESME: Darling, no-one is ever ready.

HAZEL: But I ate an entire wheel of blue cheese last night.
ESME: Hazel, I was drunk when I went into labour with your father.
HAZEL: When Nana first went into the home I started sneaking in a bottle of whiskey every visit. At three p.m. each day, she pulls it out of her little cupboard and hosts happy hour.
ESME: Your mother is going to be so excited.

Silence.

HAZEL: At Patrick and I's first hospital appointment, we meet our midwife, Trish. Things to know about Trish, in order:

She had been a midwife for thirty-something years.

She was also a part-time coach of the Central Coast twelve-year-old boys' gymnastics team.

Her office is full of trophies and medals.

Her teal tracksuit makes a swishy noise as she moves around her office and she occasionally and unexpectedly blows the whistle around her neck.

TRISH: Take your bra off, please.
HAZEL: I take off my bra and my tits drop in front of her. She has a feel of both.
TRISH: The right one is much smaller than the left. You might not be able to hold milk in that one. Something to plan for.

What's this?

HAZEL: She points at my stomach tattoo.

Ko Phangan. When I was twenty-one. I, yeah. One too many buckets.

TRISH: Ho, the places you'll go?
HAZEL: Dr Seuss.

She thrusts a pamphlet in my face.

TRISH: Any history of anxiety or depression in the family?
HAZEL: Round and round. Round and round.
TRISH: Alrighty then. We're going to have to keep an eye on that. How about your mum? Is she in your life?
HAZEL: Yeah.

I don't think Trish needs to hear the intricate details of my relationship with Clementine.

She nods, scribbles something down that I swear is a dick pic and goes to the front of the room.

TRISH: Labour is going to require flexibility, core strength, balance, upper- and lower-body strength, power, mental focus, discipline, and dedication.

HAZEL: Aren't they the eight basic skills of gymnastics?

She blows her whistle.

In the first trimester I was determined to keep the sexy times alive.

I mean, when Liv was around ten weeks pregnant, her and Justin were apparently having regular porn-star sex. And she was so damn hot. The day she told me she was pregnant, she came bouncing up the street—literally. Those titties were so delightfully full. They were up to her eyeballs. And she wasn't showing yet so she just looked like … that flame emoji. Like a mega porn star of the world.

So, on Patrick's birthday, I dressed up in a sexy maid outfit and planned to surprise him: with some role-play. I practised the script while following his movements on Find My Friends, ready to greet him at the front gate with perfect timing, Bad Bitches playlist the perfect sound design.

Hello sir, I hope you don't mind but I let myself in. I have come to do some cleaning. Of your house.

'Oh how naughty of you trespassing. You might need to be punished. Now get to work.'

Okay. What would you like me to clean first? Your … downstairs. A-area.

'Yes my downstairs area definitely needs a thorough clean. I've been wearing these pants allllll day.'

Oh well we better get those pants off quick-smart.

'I'll give your services a five-star review on Google.'

[*To audience*] We'll be better in the moment.

After sprinting back and forth from the gate several times it turns out my dodgy Wi-Fi was sending the GPS all over the place and Patrick was nowhere near where my phone said he was. My pregnant body felt like it had run a marathon.

I woke to Patrick using the feather duster prop to remove hot chip crumbs out of my cleavage.

Have sek wiht mi? [*Translation: 'Have sex with me?'*]

At fifteen weeks pregnant my boobs had shrunk. Correct, shrunk. *And* I was showing. I didn't get the memo that my body would do the opposite. No-one told me I'd look like a seventy-year-old alcoholic with man boobies.

Patrick had been googling everything. No, I'm not checking his search history, he was working from home because, pandemic, so he would use my laptop for baby googling. He was paranoid those pesky architects were tracking his productivity so he had two screens pumping like a day trader.

What happens if you have a low milk supply? Is it safe to formula-feed from birth? What colour is baby shit at birth? What is a mucus plug? How do I time contractions? How can I be a supportive partner during labour? What nappy brand is environmentally friendly? Will my cat be okay with the new addition to the family?

He was as informed as I was … not. The Google search history changed significantly when I was online.

Why are there no Uber Eats delivery partners nearby? Which is healthier—normal fries or sweet potato fries? What happened to the Honey Badger after he bailed from love on *The Bachelor*? How many times do I need to meditate a day for it to actually work?

ESME: Hazel, you need to calm the fuck down.

HAZEL: Nana used to live around the corner with Clementine. So when she worked late at the hospital on Mondays, Wednesdays and Sundays, Nana and I would have *MAFS*, Scrabble and whiskey nights. But since she moved into the home, a Covid-military-fucking fortress, they put her to bed before the sun goes down. They—

ESME: Hazel, hello, you need to calm the fuck down.

HAZEL: It was actually Nana, after doing extensive research, who whisked me and Patrick off around the twenty-five-week mark to complete the 'Relax Birth Course'—it's not enough for women to survive birth anymore, they must be relaxed while doing so?

Trish had a recent shoulder injury from attempting to rescue an overenthusiastic boy from Wyong off the pummel and couldn't lift her arm.

One of the first things she made us do was write down all of the negative associations we had with birth. Obvious words were pain and hurt and scream and death. As we called them out, Trish wrote all of the words on a whiteboard, but so far down we had to hunch forward over our bellies to read them.

I look around the class of five socially distanced couples. A young woman in the corner nudges her partner who has nodded off. Deadbeat dad alert. I look at Patrick—he is the only one with a clipboard.

TRISH: So where do you think these associations come from?

HAZEL: Um, my mother?

I look at the consensual nods around the room. It turns out that everyone in the room had a preconceived idea of birth and the majority were fucked-up stories from our mothers. Clementine has spent most of my life reminding me that the reason she has high blood pressure is because of me. Apparently she had 'textbook perfect' blood pressure her entire life up until labour. After I was born, it never went back down.

On the projector screen in front of us, a large breast appears. Trish is showing us a breastfeeding demonstration video from the eighties. Something about the boob has me on edge.

Or maybe I'm just horny.

Again.

I subtly place my hand on Patrick's leg. And move it up his thigh.

Hello second trimester happy hormones.

PATRICK: Um, Hazel what are you doing?

HAZEL: [*to audience*] I bat my eyelids. I think I am being sexy.

PATRICK: Just focus. On the boobies.

HAZEL: Just focus on these boobies.

He holds his clipboard proudly and takes notes. It's so hot.

Just as I place my hand firmly on his crotch, his phone buzzes and Trish glares at us. Patrick apologetically puts his phone on silent.

TRISH: So who here has thought about their birth plan?

HAZEL: We all nod and look at Trish eagerly: full of excitement, nerves and positivity.

Patrick is reading the text he received. I can't help but look over his clipboard. It's from Liv:

'Hey, Hazel hasn't gotten back to me about the dates for the baby shower. Also did you Google which nappy bin for the registry? Sorry I need to know sooner rather than later—before my surgery. P.S. Do you need our old cot?'

Round and round. Round and round. I didn't know they were in cahoots. And why is she getting rid of their cot? She wanted a tribe.

Trish takes me out of my thoughts:

TRISH: Birth plans are for chumps. Labour is only one day. Becoming a parent is for the rest of your life.

How do you think you're going to feel waking up every three hours for months? Then when your baby sleeps through the night for the first time and doesn't wake up? You'll be stressed. Because you will think they are dead. How are you going to feel when they shit and spew at the same time and then you shit and spew and then everyone in your household is shitting and spewing on rotation for days? How about when they walk for the first time and start grabbing for sharp objects? How are you going to feel the first time you leave them at daycare and they scream diabolically for you? How about when they go through puberty? Learn to drive? Fly to Bali for their twenty-first and call you asking for cash? Fall in love? Get heartbroken? Get married? Get divorced? Have your first grandchild?

HAZEL: I just wanted to learn how to change a nappy.

Trish hands out baby dolls. I hold mine, lovingly. Its head hits the ground with a loud thud.

Round and round. Round and round.

As I awkwardly try to reattach our baby's decapitated head, Patrick gets another text. This time, it's from Clementine. He replies:

'Sorry in birth course. Reply properly later. But have been doing my research, I think you're right, thanks so much.'

I can't say I left the Relax Birth Course, relaxed.

That was just one of many pregnancy traditions and events I did *not* enjoy.

When Liv invited me to her gender-reveal party I vomited a little in my mouth.

The party was at Liv's mum's house in Turramurra. Liv's mum Tracey was like a conservative Meryl Streep. Warm, intelligent, graceful but also like, really fucking right-wing. So it was no surprise she was clearly the brains behind this bin fire of an event.

She had contacted me a week prior, asking if I could organise the drinks.

I decide to go nek level with the job that has been bestowed upon me. Alright Tracey. You want a themed drinks table at this embarrassing bullshit event. I'll give you a drinks table at this embarrassing patriarchal bullshit event.

I decide on Long Island Iced Teas—vodka, tequila, rum, triple sec and gin. Some with pink lemonade—girls. Some with blue Gatorade—boys. And to make a point and remind everyone it's the twenty-first fucking century, a gender-neutral beverage.

I call the blue ones 'Dong Island Iced Tea'. The pink 'Long Island Iced V'. And the gender-neutral is a pinot gris.

Tracey approaches the drinks table.

TRACEY: Wow, Hazel, well done! I know Liv really appreciates the effort. I'll try an 'Iced V' and I'll grab some sort of mocktail version for Liv.

HAZEL: Mocktail? I hadn't considered that anyone would want anything that wasn't able to block their memory of the event.

I run to the bathroom and fill a plastic cup with water. On the way back I grab a blueberry from the cheese platter and throw it in.

Here you go. One Iced V and a fresh, non-alcoholic Dong … water. With blueberry. Tracey frowns at me and walks off.

The rest of the afternoon is spent running to the tap and back and dunking blueberries and raspberries into plastic cups. I am furious. I have spent days planning this Dong and V situation. I have spent expensive dollars I don't have on five different spirits. A trip to Costco to get bulk Gatorade. Meticulously pouring shots into fancy cups. I have created art. And no-one is drinking. Not even Gen and Mel. Remember my friend and her girlfriend? Well, apparently Gen is trying to get pregnant and Mel is doing that moral-support thing.

Screw you all. I'll just have to get this party going myself.

I start inhaling Dongs and Vs and gris like I'm getting paid for it.

By the time it comes to the gender reveal I am so wasted I start popping all of the blue and pink balloons with a bottle opener.

I pop each balloon with purpose. It feels good. I smile. I laugh. I pop. Pop. Pop. Pop. I notice Tracey frowning at me.

I lift the bottle opener above the random grey balloon, assuming it's some weird dud in the pack and then:

LIV: Hazel no no no no no no no that's the—

HAZEL: Pop. Blue glitter comes tumbling out, showering me and Liv. I start laughing hysterically.

Ohmyyyyygod, it's a boy! It's a boy! Liv, we're having a baby boy!

An hour later Liv is holding my head over Tracey's Turramurra toilet as blue liquid hurls out of me and hits the bottom of the sparkling bowl.

I wonderrrif he wanted aboy.

LIV: Who?

HAZEL: Dad. Maybe I was a disappointment before I was even born.

Liv strokes my hair.

Ow. She kicks me. I know, I know.

Anyway, where was I? The day after the not-so-relaxing Birth Course, Clementine asked me to meet her at home. When I walk through the front door, the first thing I notice is a box of weird old toys and Dad's ukulele in the corner of the room.

CLEMENTINE: Hazel. Don't look at me like that. It's a four-bedroom house. There is only one of me. I can't do it anymore.

Pause.

HAZEL: I am completely floored. Was she ever going to ask me if this was okay? My childhood home. A place for her granddaughter to stay. To grow up in. What about Nana's room? What about her stuff?

I look at her and all I can say is:

No wonder he never came back. Who could stand to live with such a selfish bitch.

Silence.

She is stunned by her own cruelty.

If it feels right, the actor should turn on the audience in this next moment.

[*To audience*] What? Fucking what?!

As the third trimester descended upon my mind and body, Patrick surprised me with a weekend away in Berry. A babymoon. We hid in a tiny cottage by a fireplace and ate and shagged and slept.

We decide to have a night out at a fancy restaurant and take advantage of what might be one of our last date nights for a while, with just the two of us.

As the waiter brings us our drinks, some sort of craft beer made by local hipster and a glass of French bubbles, we clink glasses and smile lovingly into each others eyes. We are that smug couple.

I take a sip of that sweet, sweet grape juice.

Out of the corner of my eye I notice two of the wait staff are looking at me. They are whispering to each other. Any fan of *Below Deck* knows that staff conversations in front of guests are a big no-no. Staff conversations *about* guests are a fireable offence.

Patrick?

PATRICK: What?

HAZEL: I think they are talking about us.

PATRICK: Who?

HAZEL: The waitress with the sleeve tat and old mate who greeted us.

PATRICK: You're being paranoid.

HAZEL: I shake it off and take another sip.

This time sleeve tat shakes her head.

See! She just. Sorry but it's my choice if I want to drink. And why does she assume I'm pregnant? I could just be a larger build. I could have eaten at the Berry Doughnut Van before we got here. It's famous Patrick, it's famous.

PATRICK: I don't think she cares. I don't even think she's looking at you. Just relax.

HAZEL: Okay, I'm sorry. Round and round. Round and round. I go to take a third sip but sort of hide the glass behind my hand like—

PATRICK: Hazel—

HAZEL: What if this is the moment I destroy my unborn child's future? What if she ends up on the streets selling her body for coke? What if this alters her brain chemistry from average-jo baby to criminal-genius jail baby? All because I couldn't wait to have a fucking glass of alcohol.

PATRICK: Hazel, we've talked about this. On the Pregnancy, Birth and Baby website it says that most of the fundamental development of the foetus occurs in the first trimester.

HAZEL: Well great, remember the blue cheese smorgasbord and two bottles of wine I consumed the night before I peed on a stick? She would have been five weeks. Five weeks! That's nearly halfway through the first trimester.

PATRICK: Yes but the What to Expect site also says that those early days are safe to—

HAZEL: Stop Googling everything Patrick!

A woman at the table next to us catches my eye.

WOMAN AT TABLE: How far along are you?

PATRICK: We're twenty-eight weeks—just hit the third trimester.

WOMAN AT TABLE: How wonderful. Do you know what you're having?

HAZEL: A girl.

WOMAN AT TABLE: Congratulations! Girls are easy babies but wait until they hit their teens.

HAZEL: Haha yep. I was one myself.

WOMAN AT TABLE: Well, all the best.

HAZEL: I take another sip and she turns back to her friend and says something.

Patrick, did you see that?

PATRICK: Okay, she was lovely and she's talking to her friend because they are at dinner together and that's what you do when you go to dinner with another human so get out of your head and talk to me. Hello, I'm here.

HAZEL: Yeah, when you're not texting Liv. Or Clementine.

PATRICK: What?

HAZEL: I know you're texting them about stuff.

PATRICK: Yes. About your baby shower. That Liv is trying to organise for you. If you replied to her, then I wouldn't have to. And you have to stop being so cruel to your mum. You haven't lived in that house for seventeen years. You have to let her move on. She's been planning to downsize for ages.

HAZEL: Sure. She hasn't done anything impulsive since she married my dad and look how that turned out.

I inhale my champagne.

Everywhere I look I see whispering nattering heads. All pointing at my belly. The glass. My belly. The glass. My belly. Round and round. Round and round.

When we return to Sydney, Patrick suggests I speak to someone about my growing anxiety. He suggests a psychologist. He suggests Headspace. But I don't need his Google suggestions.

I already know who I have to see.

MRS TWINKLES: [*now singing*] Hello everyone. Hello everyone. How are you today?

Hello everyone. Hello everyone. How are you today?

HAZEL: We're finally allowed to sing again. I let myself go.

[*Singing a little too enthusiastically*] Incy wincy spider climbed up the water spout.

It's joyful.

Down came the rain and washed poor incy out.

It's soothing.

Out came the sun and dried up all the rain so incy wincy spider climbed up the spout again!

I'm up in my own corner. I twirl my oversized jacket around. I let the lyrics infiltrate my body and my mind and my soul. I feel powerful. This is my psychologist. This is my Headspace, baby. Mrs Twinkles is my therapy!

[*A little manic*] The wheels on the bus go round and round! Round and round! Round and round! The wheels on the bus go round and round! All. Day. Long!

The room—silent parents, silent toddlers, silent tiny babies, silent Hot Dad all staring at me. I sit back down and smile. Inside, she kicks me, but I hide it well.

At the end of the session, Mrs Twinkles approaches.

MRS TWINKLES: Hazel, is it?

HAZEL: Yes, that's me! Mrs Twinkles, isn't it? It's so nice to finally—

MRS TWINKLES: Janice. My name is Janice. Look, I'm sorry to do this, but the parents have come to me and—

HAZEL: Oh, because of no masks again?

MRS TWINKLES: They've expressed concern.

HAZEL: I'm happy to wear a mask again.

MRS TWINKLES: It's not the mask. It's you.

HAZEL: Excuse me?

MRS TWINKLES: They think it's strange. That you turn up regularly. Without a child.

HAZEL: Oh. I have a child.

MRS TWINKLES: You don't. And if you do, you haven't brought them once in seven months.

HAZEL: No I'm—

MRS TWINKLES: And that jacket. There's concern for what's happening under that jacket.

HAZEL: Mrs Twinkles come on, I'm not a fucking paedophile, I'm—

MRS TWINKLES: I think it's best you leave and you don't come back.

HAZEL: I'm fucking pregnant, Janice. That's what's of concern. That's what's happening under the jacket. I am with child and I have a right to be here!

I turn and notice the parents and their kids assembled at the door, watching like gossipy hawks with too much Botox.

[*To parents*] What are you fucking looking at anyway? Or are your faces just permanently frozen. Get a better surgeon, Raelene.

MRS TWINKLES: Leave. Right now.

HAZEL: Fuck you, Janice. Or should I say, Cosima De Vito, you fried-nodule motherfucker.

MRS TWINKLES: Leave and do not come back.

HAZEL: [*to audience*] Come on. Tell her I'm not a creep. Please.

At one of my last appointments with Trish, while her fingers are inside me, she dumps a pamphlet on my belly with her other hand.

TRISH: Have you started doing the perineum massage with your partner yet?

Start it. You need to stretch the area. A head needs to fit through here. Also, make sure when you have intercourse your partner ejaculates inside you, your cervix needs to ripen.

HAZEL: From that moment on, I am like a machine. A sex robot. Despite Patrick's attempts to keep up the romance, fucking has become a technical exercise. My mind and body are in battle but I need to—

I wake up. I've been drooling on the couch when Patrick takes my hand and leads me into the bedroom.

PATRICK: Massage?

HAZEL: Perineum mas—

PATRICK: Yes, perineum massage.

HAZEL: Yep let's do it.

He's lit a candle. Jazz plays out of a small Bluetooth speaker. He has massage oil at the ready.

On the way to the bedroom I quickly print out a 'Perineum massage—how to' pack and drop the stack of paper on the bed.

Okay, this was the website the midwife recommended so I think you start by—

PATRICK: Babe, I've got this. Relax.

HAZEL: I lie down and take a deep breath.

Patrick starts massaging down my legs.

Round and round. Round and round.

It feels amazing.

He creeps up towards my lady bits. I thrust the paper in his face.

Have you read the—

PATRICK: Yes Hazel. Yes.

HAZEL: He inserts fingers and thumb and begins to slowly stretch the … region. After the burning feeling subsides, it feels … quite nice.

Breathe in. Hold. Breathe out. Breath in. Hold. Breathe out. I start to relax. Properly relax.

Oh babe. This is— (good.)

Liquid bursts out of me and directly onto Patrick's face.

I gasp.

PATRICK: Did you just piss on me?

HAZEL: Are you sure it wasn't—

PATRICK: Naaaa, that's piss.

HAZEL: We burst out laughing. He kisses me. Something about the embarrassment, his embrace and her in between us, feels incredible. We make love. I look into his eyes and say:

Make sure you ejaculate inside me, my cervix needs to ripen!

After Mrs Twinkles gave me the boot, I raged. I would hide in the bush outside the library and watch them. I'd watch Hot Dad. Raelene. Her puppet-murdering baby. And that kid with the perfect ginger hair. I became obsessed.

On one particular morning I am half an hour late for mani-pedi with Liv.

LIV: Hazel.

HAZEL: I know I know. Trish was running late at the hospital.

LIV: You're late.

HAZEL: Some woman going into labour in the car park, or something.

LIV: And you've got half a tree in your hair.

HAZEL: I shake the twigs off my head.

LIV: It's all good. I just don't have time for nails now. I've got to relieve Mum in half an hour. Maybe we can just walk?

HAZEL: Really? This mumma needs it. I want a lady to hack the dead skin off the bottom of my feet.

LIV: I can't. Maybe if you were on time, then sure.

HAZEL: Your mum will be fine! Just let her hang with Reon a bit longer.

LIV: Um, no. I've got a doctor's appointment. It's the surgery follow-up. And I have to get back and take Reon to Mini Einsteins. He is learning the recorder—

HAZEL: Yes I know. How could I forget. Deon is learning the recorder.

LIV: Reon. My son's name is Reon. And yes, he is. He loves it.

HAZEL: Of all the instruments of course Leon chooses the fucking recorder.

LIV: Hazel I might just go.

I just. I can't with you right now. I'm sorry.

HAZEL: You're not the only person to have ever had a kid, you know?

Beat.

A kid with a really shit name.

Beat.

And enough milking the endometriosis shit. Fuck, so many women have endo. It's like, the 'in' disease.

Silence.

LIV: Wow.

Grow the fuck up Hazel. I can't wait for you to have this baby. You're going to feel like a real dick. You've disappeared up your own arse. I miss my friend. I've needed you more over the last six years than ever. And you couldn't be further away. Things change. Life moves on. You're so fucking stubborn.

You've never apologised. For any of it. That first Rhyme Time … I was in the pits of newborn hell after nine months of morning sickness, years of IVF and now, this hysterectomy that's not even going to cure the shit that's going on inside me. I'm in constant pain. And I can't have any more kids, Hazel.

All I have ever wanted from you is support. But you always have to make it about yourself.

And stop being so awful to your mum. Do you really want her climbing those stairs in the middle of the night? Come on Hazel. She's in her seventies. She's just being realistic. You could try that sometime. See you at your baby shower. Don't be late.

HAZEL: As she walks away a woman in a kaftan comes up to me and touches my belly.

WOMAN IN KAFTAN: Oh mama, you are glowing—

HAZEL: I take her by the shoulders and tell her to FUCK OFF.

Fuck off and die.

The next time I see Liv is at the baby shower. My phone has been ringing non-stop since our fight, but I have been avoiding calls like the plague.

I walk nervously into Clementine's house. Into my house. Most of the furniture is gone but Liv has gone overboard. There are themed canapés and cocktails. Non-alcoholic options. A giant piñata in the shape of a baby's head. A speed-swaddle challenge. Little notes of wisdom from everyone in attendance all collated into a book. Gen and Mel have knitted her an entire wardrobe. It's so kind, but all I see when I look at the tiny knits is the baby they haven't been able to conceive over the last four and a half years of red tape and donors flaking out.

We sit in a circle and the belly and I are 'blessed'. I lift my shirt up so everyone can place one hand on it. My tattoo has now stretched across my belly. My cousin, already boozed, leans forward:

HAZEL'S COUSIN: h the places you'll g?

HAZEL: Dr Seuss. It's—

We light candles. People say nice things. Liv's mum Tracey is here, but still no sign of Clementine. Round and round. Round and round.

As the afternoon continues, I realise everyone is getting quite drunk. This time I am the sober one.

We play a game called 'Babymaker'. Photos of Patrick and I are entered into an online app. It's all projected onto a screen. The app says 'NASA is calculating the result'. I must believe the science. A horrifying image hits the screen and we all burst into laughter. It's our adult faces morphed onto a random internet image of a baby. NASA. Science.

Liv's mum, Tracey approaches, half-cut:

TRACEY: Well I haven't seen you since you made friends with the bottom of my toilet bowl!

Liv said Clementine was coming? How wonderful. She must be so proud of you.

HAZEL: I make a break for the bathroom.

Round and round.

Round and round.

On my way to the bathroom, I see the front door open. I take a deep breath. I know I need to apologise to Mum. Mum?

Two policeman walk through the door, carrying a small old-school boombox. They are wearing aviators. They are muscly. I see Liv looking at them, mouths move, they all turn and point at me.

STRIPPER COP 1: Young lady, I'm putting you under arrest.

HAZEL: They pull me over to a chair in the middle of the living room, where the entire shower has gathered to watch. They all squeal and laugh with delight. My auntie winks at me and starts threatening to get her party titty out of today's mesh-singlet special.

One of the cops hits play on the boombox and I hear those first few beats. Those famous beats of 'Pony' blast out.

Hahahaha, ohmygodohmygod Liv what have you done?

I play along. Round and round. Round and round.

They gyrate. They flip. They spin. They perform the rotating porpoise. I hold their buttocks like I held Major Vincent's. My heart is racing.

They get down to the moment of truth—their pants are coming off. Right as Ginuwine hits the chorus they thrust their crutches forward and whip their pants off in a flash to reveal …

Nappies?

What the—

They are wearing nappies.

STRIPPER COP 2: Mummy, my bum-bum is dirty.

HAZEL: Round and round.

STRIPPER COP 1: Mummy could you change my nappy?

HAZEL: Round and round.

STRIPPER COP 1: Dirty bum-bum—

HAZEL: I'm not sure I want—

Both cops whip off their nappies and their arses are covered in shit. I gag. Tracey leaves the room. Laughter echoes through the space. I want to …

One of them leans down and whispers:

STRIPPER COP 2: It's okay, it's Nutella. You're safe. Do you give us permission?

HAZEL: Before I have a chance to say I don't like Nutella, my face gets wedged between both Nutella-covered buttcheeks. They are motorboating my face. Round and round. Round and round. She's kicking me. Kick. Kick. Kick. Kick. I can't. I. I am drowning. Where am I?

I see kaftan woman. Her manicured fingers on my belly.

Major Vincent. He is laughing at my body?

Turtleneck touches me. They laugh.

Trish is holding my wonky, small breast.

They recoil.

Am I disgusting? Will my vagina will be destroyed? Will I ever be sexy again?

Oh God … Liv …

Who have I become? Your own mother doesn't want to be near you.

Round and round. Round and round.

Dad's voice. That's my dad. He is singing. I can't see him but I can hear him.

Kick kick kick kick.

Stop it. Fucking stop it! That hurts! This is my body! Mine! Get out! Get out of me!

Silence.

The guilt … the guilt is.

And then I hear a strum. A ukulele strum. One of the strippers has Dad's ukulele. He begins to play along to 'Pony'.

I feel piss stream down my leg.

Silence.

Liv wipes Nutella off my face in the bathroom.

I look out the bathroom window and think: Nutella isn't as bad as I remember it.

That night I tell Patrick the story. He holds me and says:

PATRICK: Keep talking to that therapist. You're going to be the most amazing mum.

HAZEL: I agree. I need to go back to therapy.

She is back in the present.

MRS TWINKLES: [*spoken*] Hello everyone. Hello everyone. How are you today? Hello everyone. Hello everyone. How are you today?

HAZEL: Mrs Twinkles delivers this weeks ‘Hello’ song directly to me. It’s been a month, and she’s welcomed me back. She looks at me warmly. I take a deep breath. I remove my jacket. Finally. She almost cracks a smile. She’s not as uncomfortable and concerned about my presence as she was when she booted my arse. She looks at my belly. She’s on show. Hello everyone.

Kick.

As she opens up that caterpillar book, another Rhyme Time classic, I shuffle in my seat. Everything feels a bit …

She feels underneath herself.

My phone vibrates. I look down to see if it’s Liv. I’m now running late for our coffee. It’s not. Mrs Twinkles frowns.

The number stops ringing and my phone is still open on a web page with different colours of vaginal discharge.

MRS TWINKLES: On Tuesday he ate—

HAZEL: Vibrating. My phone keeps vibrating. Private number. Please go away.

MRS TWINKLES: On Thursday he ate through five blueberrries—

HAZEL: It rings again. I have to answer. I’ll tell them to delete my number and never contact me again. I sneak to the back of the room.

Hello?

CLEMENTINE: Hazel?

HAZEL: Mum?

Mrs Twinkles is not impressed.

Mum. Why is your number private?

Round and round.

Round and round.

CLEMENTINE: Because of work. Listen, Hazel. It’s Nana. They’ve moved her from the geriatric ward to cardiac.

Silence.

You should get there as soon as possible.

HAZEL: Can she still host happy hour?

CLEMENTINE: Hazel, she's not. I don't. I don't know.

HAZEL: I get all the details. She's at the cardiac ward at RPA She's been there since Saturday, the day of the baby shower.

I go back to my seat in the corner.

I take a deep breath.

I start singing.

The wheels on the bus go round and round. Round and round. Round and round.

The wheels on the bus go round and round. All. Day. Long.

She's kicking me. She's kicking in time.

Round and round! Round and round!

Ow. I grab my belly. I lean forward. I'm sweating. I think I'm having a panic attack.

I gasp. I'm struggling to breathe.

MRS TWINKLES: Okay everyone I think we'll end it right there. Leave the cushions and puppets where they are.

Hazel, are you okay?

How many weeks are you?

Hazel, take deep breaths. How far along are you?

Just calm down. Breathe. You're okay. Can I borrow your phone?

HAZEL: [*to audience*] Have I been singing out loud?

I need to go to the hospital. I need to see my nana.

I hand her my phone. I can't hear anything clearly anymore. Pins and needles run up my arms. It's like my head is static on a television screen. My ears whistle. I cover them. Kick kick kick kick. The pain is low. I put my hands against the wall. Mrs Twinkles voice fades in and out of the room. I hear her saying Liv's name.

MRS TWINKLES: I'm with your friend Hazel. Yes, Mrs Twinkles from Glebe Rhyme Time. Yeah, she's been coming for months. Oh. Okay. Yes, yep. Months. You can call me Janice. Look Hazel is in a complete state. I'm going to drive her to the—Yep. Okay. Great. Tell him we'll be there in twenty to thirty minutes. Fab. See you soon.

HAZEL: As she locks up the old wooden door and we head to her car, I start to calm down. I am in safe hands, with Janice.

MRS TWINKLES: Have you got any pain?

HAZEL: Just occasional stabs. Quite low.

MRS TWINKLES: Braxton Hicks probably. I have two teenage girls. Just keep breathing.

HAZEL: I'm sorry, I'm a bit embarrassed.

MRS TWINKLES: It's okay. You don't have to explain. I've called your friend Liv. And she's calling your husband. Is there anyone else I should contact?

HAZEL: —

MRS TWINKLES: Would you like me to call Raelene?

HAZEL: Sorry, what?

MRS TWINKLES: [*doing Botox face and voice*] I said Raelene. Would you like me to call Raelene?

HAZEL: [*laughing*] Oh, that's. That's brilliant.

MRS TWINKLES: Too much money. Not enough brains.

HAZEL: You're awful Janice!

MRS TWINKLES: Well, she's a cunt.

HAZEL: I always knew Janice was a woman of integrity.

Did Liv say she was coming? With Reon?

MRS TWINKLES: Fucking stupid name. It's a spelling mistake. I thought she said Leon the first time I—

HAZEL: Me too Janice. Me too.

I—

Ugh. She's kickboxing in the womb. I can't. Ah. Sorry.

MRS TWINKLES: Just breathe.

HAZEL: We pull up at RPA Liv and Patrick are waiting out the front.

MRS TWINKLES: Just remember, round and round. Round and fucking round.

HAZEL: She puts on a pair of sunnies, cranks the radio and speeds off like a sixteen-year-old who just got mufflers on their wheels.

Patrick and Liv take me to the main desk to find Nana's ward. Occasionally I have to stop because of the Toni Braxton Hicks. I tell Liv it's okay, she's doesn't have to be here, I'm fine now. She insists on staying.

LIV: Anything to get away from that fucking recorder.

HAZEL: I grab her hand and she squeezes it. We head up to the cardiac ward. Liv and Patrick aren't allowed in Nana's room. They wait outside.

I quietly open the door and turn the corner.

Nana?

Nana?

Nana.

She's not. Why can't she … ? Pins and needles start running up my arms again. Static in my head. My breath is short. I gasp. I can't get enough air. Round and round. Round and round.

ESME: Hazel. For goodness' sake girl, why didn't you say you were here?

HAZEL: Nana. Hi. Nana. How are you?

ESME: Do you really want me to answer that?

HAZEL: She leans down towards the little cupboard next to her bed and gets out a bottle of whiskey.

ESME: Tipple?

HAZEL: It's not happy hour yet.

ESME: Every hour is happy hour.

HAZEL: I can't Nana.

She takes a swig of whiskey.

ESME: You're huge.

HAZEL: I know. And I just had an attack of that Toni Braxton Hicks thing, I think they've stopped. And Nana the stuff coming out of me.

ESME: It's like a Jackson Pollock painting in your knickers.

Silence.

HAZEL: What if I don't know how to do it?

ESME: No-one knows how to do it. You learn on the job.

Silence.

HAZEL: Remember that apartment I moved into in third-year uni? Liv gave me a succulent. The plant you give to people because they are apparently super-easy to look after? Well, I killed it. I managed to kill an unkillable plant. I kill plants. I kill dicks. How on earth am I going to keep a baby alive?

ESME: Well you will because you don't have a choice.

HAZEL: Yeah I guess.

Silence.

Nana I get stuck.

It might sound stupid, but there's part of me that's hoping he'll come home.

But then I remember it's been twenty-eight years.

[*To audience*] And I've been stuck in this thought for twenty-eight years.

The only thing that brings me comfort are the songs he sang.

How can I bring this thing into a world that he's not in? It makes no sense. What if I am already like him? What if I have this baby and one day I just leave?

ESME: Some things in life will never make sense. I've never understood why he left and I don't think I ever will. But you're not him. You are loyal. And you are stubborn to the point that you could never just leave. Just like your mother. You're just like her.

And if all else fails, drink some whiskey. It makes everything better.

HAZEL: Can I … ?

I take a swig of whiskey and give the bottle back.

A nurse walks in. It's the same nurse who was in emergency when I killed all those dicks. I try to hide behind a small chair and pull my hair across my face.

[*To audience*] Am I attempting to create the illusion of a moustache?

RPA NURSE: Esme, blood-pressure check.

HAZEL: She looks at me. She gestures towards my belly.

RPA NURSE: Ah, it worked out for you then?

HAZEL: Apparently so.

She gives me a nod and leaves.

Silence.

Nana you know Mum sold the house—

ESME: Of course I do. I actually speak to her Hazel.

You've got to cut her some slack.

She's thrilled about becoming a grandmother. And you're taking that away from her.

HAZEL: I'm not. She hasn't. She doesn't consider me in any of it.

ESME: Grow up Hazel. She stayed in that stupid old rickety house for three decades for you. Fuck those stairs. Since she pushed you out of her moot she has been considering you—

HAZEL: Moot? Really?

ESME: Hazel where do you think the cot came from? And all of the baby business Patrick has been collecting? It's your old stuff. Clementine saved it all.

HAZEL: I didn't ask her to do that.

ESME: She doesn't need another family member disappearing on her.
Nurse can you please get her out of here? She's in labour.

HAZEL: I'm not. It's Toni Braxton Hicks.

ESME: Her waters have broken.

HAZEL: And just like that I'm whisked out of the room. I turn back. The nurse is confiscating her bottle of whiskey. Nana is yelling at her.
Patrick and Liv take me down to the Women and Babies unit.

LIV: I'll call your mum. I'm so proud of you. And excited. You've got this.

HAZEL: She leaves.
Trish greets us. The whistle is around her neck.

TRISH: Okay, let's get you up on the horse and check out what this mystery liquid is all about.

HAZEL: As she shoves a speculum up me, she talks about the various stages of labour and the equipment Patrick and I can use throughout.

TRISH: We'll be on the floor, the horse, the still rings, the vault, the parallel bars and the horizontal bar.

HAZEL: Two doctors come in and join her. They all stare up my vagina.

TRISH: Cough please.

HAZEL: I cough and liquid comes pouring out of me.
Trish blows her whistle.

TRISH: Those waters are well and truly broken. You'll be having a baby today.

HAZEL: The pins and needles come back. Static in my head. The room spins. I am overcome with heat.
Sorry, I feel a bit. I just need to sit.
Trish takes my blood pressure. It's apparently high. Higher than they'd like. The doctors want to run some extra tests. Nothing to worry about, they say.
They hook me up to a machine. We can hear her heartbeat. It's perfect. She's right there.

TRISH: Look you've developed something we call severe pre-eclampsia. Did you say you've been feeling a bit light-headed? It's nothing to worry about, but your kidneys and liver are starting to fail. She's fine, you're fine, but we gotta get this girl out sooner rather than later.

HAZEL: My mum had pre-eclampsia. With me.

TRISH: Well there you go. The apple doesn't fall far from the tree.

HAZEL: As Patrick sets up our Bluetooth speaker and fairy lights, Trish brings in Tim the epidural man. She explains they have to give me an epidural because they can't let my blood pressure rise. I think about the Relax Birth Course and the prep we'd done for a 'natural birth'. I have no choice but to have an epidural? Oh no. What a shame.

Bring it Tim. Gimme that sweet sweet jab.

TIM: Now Hazel, in order to test the effectiveness of the epidural we run some ice along your skin. When you can feel the pressure but not the cold, let me know.

HAZEL: He leans over me in the hospital bed and slowly runs an ice cube from my chest down to my thigh.

TIM: Here?

HAZEL: Cold.

TIM: How about here?

HAZEL: Still cold.

TIM: Okay I'm going to go a little lower. Here?

HAZEL: Oh that's good.

PATRICK: Hazel!

HAZEL: Sorry it just, it tickles. It feels nice. It's … sexy.

PATRICK: Hazel!

HAZEL: I start laughing. So does Patrick.

TIM: Okay, it shouldn't tickle here.

HAZEL: That's numb. It's not cold. Its just … pressure. Fuck, that's weird.

Tim leaves to the sounds of a woman screeching profanities next door.

I realise I probably won't feel pain like that. Having an epidural at the start of labour is like being paralysed.

At midnight Trish leaves me hooked up to the oxytocin drip as it slowly brings on my contractions. I occasionally hit the button on the epidural for a top-up. I can't move. I stare at the ceiling listening to her heartbeat.

Patrick, we're having a baby.

PATRICK: We are.

HAZEL: He closes his eyes and nods off in the chair. I try to sleep but can't. Every half an hour Trish comes back in the room to check my blood pressure. I talk her ear off about everything. Then she leaves and I stare at the ceiling. Round and round. Round and round.

I stare at my phone. I Google pre-eclampsia. I start to read horror stories and then stop. I scroll aimlessly through Instagram. I go to my voicemails. I haven't checked them for a couple of weeks. The last one is from the day of my baby shower.

CLEMENTINE: Hazel, darling. Have you been getting my messages? Look, I'm so sorry but I'm not going to make it today. It's Esme. The home have called and she needs to go to hospital. She's just going into the geriatric ward for observation. I'm on my way there now. Neither of us want you to worry. Just have the most wonderful time. Liv has gone all out. Anyway, I'm sorry. And please call me. When you can.

HAZEL: I think about Mum putting her body through this. I imagine her lying in a hospital bed listening to my heartbeat.

Twelve hours later Trish has my knees up, my legs spread and is looking up my vagina with a heavy-duty torch. She has ten fingers inside me.

TRISH: Tens across the board. We are fully dilated. Hospital protocol is we give you two hours to push.

HAZEL: Then what happens?

TRISH: Then we bring in the big guns. But don't you worry about that yet. Remember, we're using flexibility, core strength, balance, upper- and lower-body strength, power, mental focus, discipline, and dedication.

HAZEL: She blows her whistle.

I start pushing. Or I think I am pushing. I am still numb from the epidural, which Trish has now turned off so I can work with the contractions, but it's really hard to know if I'm using the right muscles. Or pushing in the right way. Patrick holds my hand the whole time. He is calm.

TRISH: Push down. Dowwwwwwn. Like you're taking the biggest shit of your life.

HAZEL: I am tryiiiing. I can't feel. When I push, I can't feel where down is.

I am giving this everything I've got. Round and round. Round and round. I'm sorry—

PATRICK: Stop apologising.

HAZEL: Sorry, I'll stop. Apologising.

An ad for Royal Casino comes blasting through the Bluetooth speaker. Should have paid for premium.

TRISH: Work with those contractions. Breathe and push down. Focus. Discipline. Dedication.

PATRICK: Hazel, I can see her head. I can see her little head.

HAZEL: Patrick is down with Trish looking up my vagina with the heavy-duty torch.

TRISH: Come on Hazel. Breathe and push. Breathe and push. She wants to come.

HAZEL: Sorry sorry sorry sorry I am trying. I am pushing. I can't feel where down is. Am I shitting? I'm so sorry.

PATRICK: Stop apologising—

HAZEL: Sorry, oh shit, I've shat haven't I? Did I shit? Work with the contractions. Discpline. Focus. Sorry did I miss one? Ahhh sorry. Did I poo? I've pooed. I haven't? Sorry I've definitely shat. Haven't I? Oh fuck um I'm sort of feeling the pain now. Ohmyfuckinggodholyfuckbuttsinhell sorry sorry sorry!

Just as it is becoming too much, as the epidural wears off and I decide I can't do this anymore, I look deep into Patrick's eyes and command: Playlist Bad Bitches. Play it. Now.

And out of the speakers blasts 'Pony'.

I breathe. And push. And sing.

She sings the chorus of 'Pony' by Ginuwine.

Patrick joins in. So does Trish.

She sings the chorus again.

TRISH: She's coming. Hazel she's coming. You've got one more in you. I know you do. You've got this.

HAZEL: I breathe and push.

I think about Nana. I think about Mum. I think about all the women who have done this before me.

And then … And then … A sound I can never run away from. The lights become brighter and more colourful until:

HAZEL *holds a little bundle. She rocks it back and forth.*

Hello Esme.

[*Singing softly*] The wheels on the bus go round and round, round and round, round and round. The wheels on the bus go round and round, all day long.

For the first time in the play, HAZEL *is now able to move on to the second verse.*

The wipers on the bus go swish swish swish. Swish swish swish …

As HAZEL *continues to sing, softly, gently and possibly now in tune, a recorded version of 'The Wheels on the Bus' starts to play. As it gets louder and louder:*

Blackout.

THE END

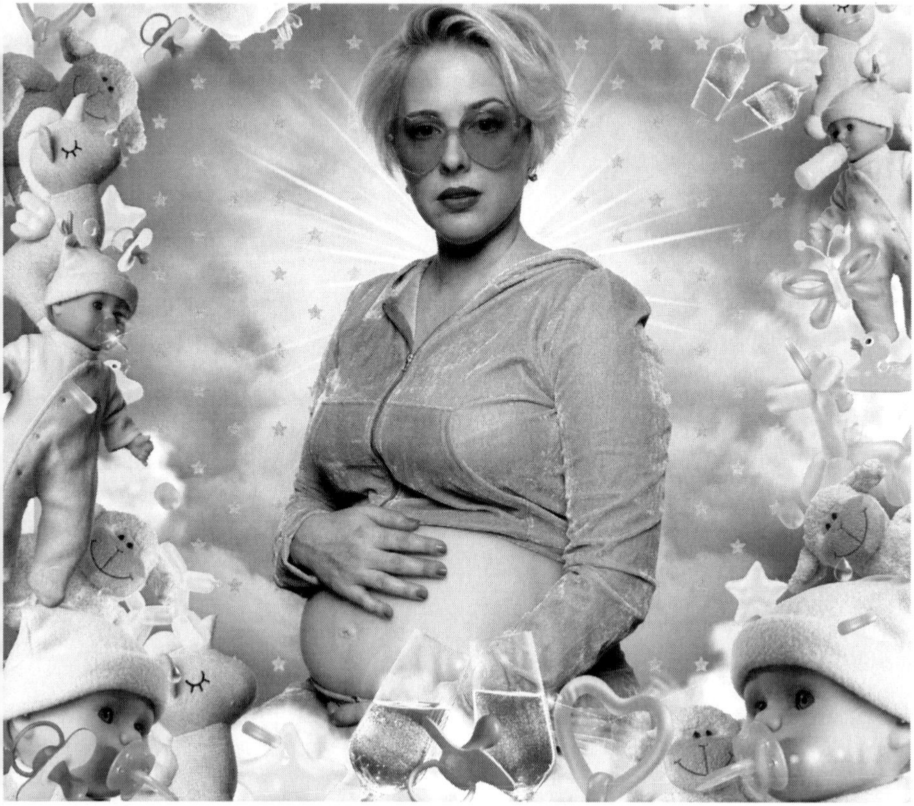

GRIFFIN THEATRE COMPANY PRESENTS

PONY

BY ELOISE SNAPE

12 MAY – 17 JUNE 2023 | SBW STABLES THEATRE

GRIFFIN
THEATRE
COMPANY

Government partners

This production of *Pony* was supported through a residency at Theatre and Performance Studies, the University of Sydney.

CAST & CREATIVES

Director **Anthea Williams**

Production Designer **Isabel Hudson**

Lighting Designer **Verity Hampson**

Composer & Sound Designer **Me-Lee Hay**

Stage Manager **Jen Jackson**

With
Briallen Clarke

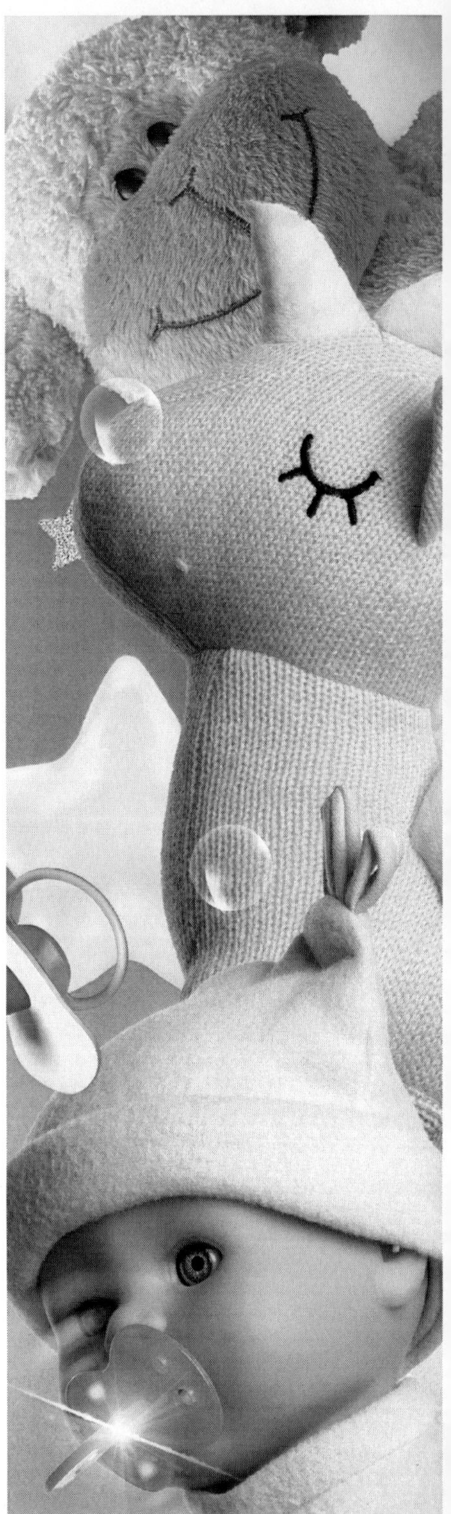

Griffin acknowledges the generosity of the Seaborn, Broughton & Walford Foundation in allowing it the use of the SBW Stables Theatre rent free, less outgoings, since 1986.

PLAYWRIGHT'S NOTE

During one of the final developments of this play, in a room at Griffin with **Anthea Williams** and **Julian Larnach**, after much discussion and dancing with the whiteboard, we realised that *Pony* is really, at its core, a story about the impossibility of the journey to becoming a mother. *Impossible* feels like a bit of a hectic word to use, but when you break it down, it's a pretty good description.

Labour is exceptionally demanding, physically and mentally—it is literally life-threatening, and the expectations on this generation of parents are intense. We are expected to grow humans in our bodies, raise them without screwing them up, continue to hold down successful, meaningful careers and relationships, all while keeping our mental health intact and presenting to the world as though we are really, really enjoying ourselves. Surely this is kind of... impossible? And yet every day around the world, babies are born. Throw a pandemic in the mix and well—it's wild. The irony is that the pandemic, while of course devastating and difficult (that goes without saying), wasn't nearly as weird as what was happening to my body while I was pregnant.

This was the original seed of the idea that this play was born from (sorry, sorry—birth puns). I started to write in the final weeks of my own pregnancy and then my thoughts spiralled into a story once my beautiful daughter Winnie was born. In the midst of lockdowns, exhaustion and anxiety, I didn't have much of a filter, so my ideas felt honest and raw. I was in shock in those early weeks of motherhood—which of course everyone tells you to prepare for, but again, that is *impossible.* I tried to sell a version of 'I'm totally fine' to those around me—to my closest friends and family—even to those who were going through the exact same thing. Why couldn't I be honest about my experience? Maybe this play is my attempt to do that.

My hope is that I have written a story that is relatable. A deeply flawed character who is human and real. And that I've represented a variety of experiences and ideas around the often treacherous, difficult, but ultimately hopeful experience that is the journey to becoming a parent. I hope audiences are able to laugh—properly laugh—as Hazel navigates her fears. Her fear of change, her fear of not knowing herself anymore, her fear of losing herself completely.

I am so thankful for the incredible brains that have created this story with me. Having never written a play before, it's clear that I needed them. I'm thankful to **Frieda Lee** and **Adrienne Patterson**—who encouraged me to pursue the idea when I was right in the thick of what felt like a newborn baby had given me a lobotomy. To Julian Larnach for your positivity and guiding me through the playwriting process while throwing in what I reckon are some of the funniest jokes in the play. To Declan and the Griffin folk for taking a chance on me as a writer and for working insanely hard in one of the toughest industries through one of the toughest times. To the magnificent **Briallen Clarke**—my mate Bri. I still pinch myself daily that you said yes to bringing this to life. What a magical experience to do this with you. And to

Anthea Williams, who has developed *Pony* with me from the beginning. Your heart is beating behind this story. You know how important you are—your unwavering faith in me and Hazel is the reason this play has found a home and I truly believe your genius is unmatched.

And finally to those who I would not be alive without: thank you to my Mum, my Dad, my husband Sam, my cat Terrence and of course, my daughter Winnie, who *Pony* is dedicated to.

The fear that I would lose myself didn't become a reality. In fact, when you came along, the opposite happened.

Eloise Snape
Playwright

DIRECTOR'S NOTE

Elo and I started working on *Pony* during the first lockdown via Zoom. I'd taken over the care of my folks, so often Elo had baby Winnie cooing in the background, while I had elderly parents wandering in asking what was for dinner and how to get 'that *Crown* show' back on the TV. This is the everyday care that so often falls to women as we lead our multiplicitous lives.

Eloise is one of the most generous people you could meet, and this generosity extends to sharing her personal and emotional life. Eloise and I discussed everything from the day to day of how to get a coffee during a pandemic to our physical and mental health, including our sex lives (sorry Sam and Tim), and how we'd made, or tried to make, decisions around having children.

Then slowly we'd segue into the heart of who this woman Hazel is, and what she is dealing with. We slowly came to see *Pony* as a coming-of-middle-age story. What to do when you desperately want to be young and free, but if you don't move into the next phase of your life, you might never have the chance to. Also, no matter what you decide about children, you can't stop your parents and grandparents from getting older—time is a great villain.

Eloise is one of these glorious people who can find joy always, yet she feels everything. You can make her laugh and cry with a single sentence. As much as anything, this is where Hazel comes from. She's a woman who wants to suck the marrow out of life, even if she's having a mental breakdown at the same time.

But where Hazel can be lacking in insight, Elo has laser vision.

So as I walk into rehearsals with a brilliant team, for a fabulous theatre company and with the wonderful **Briallen Clarke** about to shine in the role of Hazel, I am thinking about all of these facets that put together a meaningful life. How do we suck all the gritty, human joy out of this life? How do we face the light while making sure we feel it, and face it all? How do we grow into the next version of ourselves while looking after those we love?

Anthea Williams
Director

BIOGRAPHIES

ELOISE SNAPE
PLAYWRIGHT

Eloise is an award-winning writer, actor, producer and voice artist. She completed a Bachelor of Media in Writing at Macquarie University and received a scholarship to study in London. She also attended Actors Centre Australia and holds an Advanced Diploma of Performing Arts majoring in Acting. Eloise has worked extensively as an actor in theatre and she works consistently on screen, most recently in *Colin from Accounts* for CBS/Binge and *Voice Activated*. As a producer, she has worked with her own independent theatre company, MopHead Productions, as well as Ensemble Theatre and Griffin Theatre Company. She is currently a Creative Producer with Critical Stages. Eloise's debut work as a writer, *Pony*, was shortlisted for the Queensland Premier's Drama Award 2022/23, the Rodney Seaborn Playwrights Award 2021, the Patrick White Playwright's Award 2022 and the Griffin Award 2022.

ANTHEA WILLIAMS
DIRECTOR

Anthea Williams is an award-winning theatre director and an emerging film director. She is a Churchill Fellow and develops both theatre and screen writing. Anthea's directing credits include: for Griffin/Sydney Festival: *Since Ali Died*; for Belvoir: *Cinderella*, *Forget Me Not*, *Hir*, *Kill the Messenger*, *Old Man*, *Winyanboga Yurringa*; for Black Cat National/UK Tours: *Mother's Ruin*; for the Bush Theatre (UK): *50 Ways to Leave Your Lover*, *suddenlossofdignity.com*, *The Great British Country Fete*, *Two Cigarettes*, *Turf*; for Carriageworks: *Sleeplessness*; for the Court (Aotearoa/New Zealand): *The Pink Hammer*; for National Theatre of Parramatta: *Flight Paths*, *Things I Could Never Tell Steven*; for NIDA: *#KillAllMen*, *Love and Information*, *The Colby Sisters of Pittsburgh, Pennysylvania*; for Red Line Productions at the Old Fitz: *The Humans*; and for UTP: *M'ap Boulé*. From 2011 – 2017, Anthea was Literary Manager then Associate Director – New Work at Belvoir. From 2007 – 2011, she was Associate Director – bushfutures at London's Bush Theatre. Anthea's short film *Safety Net* was part of the official selection for the Sydney Film Festival, Slamdance Festival and was shortlisted for Whānāu Marama— the New Zealand International Film Festival's Best Short Award.

ISABEL HUDSON
SET & COSTUME DESIGNER

Isabel is an award-winning set and costume designer. Isabel's design credits for the stage include: for Griffin: *Ghosting the Party*; for Belvoir: *Blessed Union*, *Every Brilliant Thing*, *Winyanboga Yurringa*; for Belvoir 25A: *Jess & Joe Forever*, *Tuesday*; for Hayes Theatre Co: *Razorhurst, The View Upstairs*; for Melbourne Theatre Company: *Torch the Place*; for New Theatricals: *Darkness*; for NIDA: *Mr Burns*; for Pinchgut Opera: *Farnace*; for Sydney Festival/Rising/Darwin Festival: *Maureen: Harbinger of Death*; and for Sydney

Theatre Company: *Hubris & Humiliation*. Isabel's set design credits include: for Hayes Theatre Co: *American Psycho*, *Cry-Baby*, *Young Frankenstein*. She was the costume designer and associate set designer for *The Mousetrap* (Crossroads Productions). Isabel has won the Sydney Theatre Award for Best Set Design of an Independent Production two years in a row—for the musicals *American Psycho* and *Cry-Baby* at Hayes Theatre Co, which went on to tour to the Sydney Opera House. Isabel also won the APDG Award for Best Set Design for *American Psycho*. Isabel is the Australian Set Associate for *Moulin Rouge! The Musical* Australia, Korea and Japan. She was recently awarded the Kristian Fredrikson Scholarship and the Thelma Louise Award. Isabel holds a Bachelor of Design from NIDA and a Bachelor of Arts (Screen and Sound) from the University of New South Wales.

VERITY HAMPSON

LIGHTING DESIGNER

Verity's lighting designs for theatre include: for Griffin: *A Strategic Plan*, *And No More Shall We Part*, *Angela's Kitchen*, *Beached*, *Dealing With Clair*, *Dogged*, *Ghosting the Party*, *Orange Thrower*, *The Bleeding Tree*, *The Boys*, *The Bull*, *The Moon and the Coronet of Stars*, *The Floating World*, *Superheroes*, *This Year's Ashes*, *The Turquoise Elephant*; for Griffin Independent: *The Brothers Size*, *The Cold Child*, *Crestfall*, *Family Stories: Belgrade*, *Live Acts On Stage*, *Music*, *The New Electric Ballroom*, *References to Salvador Dali Make Me Hot*, *Way to Heaven*; for Griffin/Bell Shakespeare: *The Literati*; for Bell Shakespeare: *A Midsummer Night's Dream*, *Julius Caesar*, *Titus Andronicus*; for Belvoir: *An Enemy of the People*, *The Blind Giant is Dancing*, *The Drover's Wife*, *Faith Healer*, *Ivanov*, *Sami in Paradise*, *Winyanboga Yurringa*; for Black Swan/Sydney Theatre Company: *City of Gold*; for CAAP/Sydney Festival: *Double Delicious*; for Dancenorth: *Dungarri Nya Nya*; for Ensemble Theatre: *A Doll's House*, *Baby Doll*, *Fully Committed*, *The One*; for Hayes Theatre Co: *Lizzie*; for Malthouse Theatre: *Wake in Fright*; for Queensland Theatre: *Death of a Salesman*; and for Sydney Theatre Company: *7 Stages of Grieving*, *A Raisin in the Sun*, *Blackie Blackie Brown*, *Fences*, *Grand Horizons*, *Hamlet: Prince of Skidmark*, *Home, I'm Darling*, *Machinal*, *Little Mercy*. Verity is a recipient of the Mike Walsh Fellowship and has won three Sydney Theatre Awards, a Green Room Award and an APDG Award for Best Lighting Design.

ME-LEE HAY

COMPOSER & SOUND DESIGNER

Me-Lee Hay composes for film, television, dance and theatre. A Malaysian born Chinese-Australian, she has had works shown across many platforms including Netflix, Australian commercial TV channels and at mainstream cinemas. Off screen, Me-Lee's credits as composer & sound designer include: for Monkey Baa Theatre: *Little Bozu and Kon Kon*; for National Theatre of Parramatta: *Guards at the Taj*, *Launchpad*; for Sydney Dance Company PPY: *Elastic Stasis*, *Orfeo ed Euridice*, *To the Foreign Void and Back*; for Sydney Theatre Company: *White Pearl*. She has toured to the UK to work as composer, music director and musician on *Things Hidden Since the Foundation of World* for The Javaad Alipoor Company and National Theatre of Parramatta. She was composer and performing musician in Q Theatre's *Yellow Yellow Sometimes Blue*. Classically trained in piano and cello, Me-Lee is a graduate of the Australian Film

Television & Radio School (AFTRS), is an Associate Composer Representative of the Australian Music Centre and is the Vice President of the Australian Guild of Screen Composers. She is published by Gaga music.

JEN JACKSON

STAGE MANAGER

Jen Jackson (she/her) is a Korean-Australian stage manager, living and working on Gadigal land, with a particular passion for new Australian work and a commitment to diversity in theatre. After attending UNSW in a Bachelor of Arts majoring in Theatre & Performance, she continued her studies at NIDA with a degree in Technical Theatre & Stage Management. Recent productions she has stage managed include: for Griffin: *Golden Blood (黃金血液)*, *End Of.*; for Contemporary Asian Australian Performance: *Double Delicious*; for Kurinji/SAtheCollective: *宿 (stay)*; and for National Theatre of Parramatta: *Nothing*. Recently, Jen was company manager for National Theatre of Parramatta's *Choir Boy* (Sydney WorldPride and NSW/ACT Tour). Jen hopes to help bring to life stories of all kinds that challenge, entertain, reflect, make us feel, think, and examine ourselves—the kind of stuff that made her fall in love with theatre in the first place.

BRIALLEN CLARKE

HAZEL

Briallen is an acting graduate of the National Institute of Dramatic Art. Television credits include: for ABC: *Fresh Blood*, *The Heights*; for Matchbox Pictures/Peacock: *Irreverent*; for Nine Network: *Doctor Doctor*; and for 7mate: *Australia's Sexiest Tradie*. On stage, Briallen originated the role of Joanie in the highly acclaimed world premiere of *Muriel's Wedding the Musical* for Global Creatures and Sydney Theatre Company. Other credits include: for Griffin: *A Strategic Plan*, *Rapid Write: Hollywood Ending*; for Darlinghurst Theatre Company: *All My Sons*, *The Lunch Hour*, *The Young Tycoons*; for Ensemble Theatre: *Clybourne Park*, *The Plant*; for Sydney Theatre Company: *Hay Fever*; for Melbourne Arts Centre: *Dreamsong*; and for the Old Fitz; *Pork Stiletto*. Briallen also co-produced Australian Theatre for Young People's highly acclaimed production of *Stop Kiss*. Briallen is dedicating her performance in *Pony* to her late teacher and beloved theatre doyen, Kevin Jackson.

ABOUT GRIFFIN

Griffin is the only theatre company in the country exclusively devoted to the development and staging of new Australian writing. Located in the historic SBW Stables Theatre, nestled in the heart of Kings Cross, Griffin has been Australia's home for the exploration of new stories since 1978.

We are the launch pad for new plays, ideas and writing that other theatres won't take a risk on. We boldly contribute to Australia's unique and powerful storytelling culture. Plays like *Prima Facie*, *Holding the Man* and *City of Gold* all had their world premieres at Griffin before going out to capture the national imagination. In the words of our longest-serving Artistic Director, **Ros Horin**:

"We are the theatre of first chances."

We are passionate about nurturing emerging and established practitioners alike. We pride ourselves on supporting our vast community of artists, audiences and supporters who consider our theatre their creative home. We help ambitious, bold, risk-taking and urgent Australian work get from the page onto the stage. We tell the stories that help us know who we are as a nation, and who we want to become.

Acknowledgement of Country

Griffin Theatre Company and the SBW Stables Theatre operate and tell stories on the unceded lands of the Gadigal of the Eora Nation. We acknowledge and honour Aboriginal and Torres Strait Islander people as the oldest continuous living culture on the planet, with more than 60,000 years of storytelling practice shaping and underpinning all aspects of Australian culture. It is a privilege that we do not take lightly: to work on this land, and to tell stories on its soil.

GRIFFIN THEATRE COMPANY
13 Craigend St
Kings Cross NSW 2011

02 9332 1052
info@griffintheatre.com.au
griffintheatre.com.au

SBW STABLES THEATRE
10 Nimrod St
Kings Cross NSW 2011

BOOKINGS
griffintheatre.com.au
02 9361 3817

GRIFFIN FAMILY

Patron
Seaborn, Broughton & Walford Foundation

Griffin acknowledges the generosity of the Seaborn, Broughton & Walford Foundation in allowing it the use of the SBW Stables Theatre rent free, less outgoings, since 1986.

Board
Bruce Meagher (Chair)
Guillaume Babille
Simon Burke AO
Julieanne Campbell
Lyndell Droga
Declan Greene
Nakul Legha
Julia Pincus
Lenore Robertson
Simone Whetton

Artistic Director & CEO
Declan Greene

Executive Director & CEO
Julieanne Campbell

General Manager
Khym Scott

Associate Artistic Director
Andrea James

Literary Manager (Acting)
Julian Larnach

Box Office Manager
Gary Barker

Ticketing Administrator
Nathan Harrison

Bar Manager
Alex Bryant-Smith

Front of House
Riordan Berry, Kandice Joy, Max Philips, Willo Young

Head of Development
Jake Shavikin

Relationships Manager
Ell Katte

Finance Manager
Kylie Richards

Finance Consultant
Emma Murphy

Marketing Manager
Erica Penollar

Content Producer
Ang Collins

Senior Producer
Leila Enright

Ticketing & Administration Coordinator
Kate Marks

Strategic Insights Consultant
Peter O'Connell

Sustainability Coordinators
Ang Collins, Julian Larnach

Brand & Graphic Design
Alphabet

Web Developer
DevQuoll

Cover Photography
Brett Boardman

GRIFFIN DONORS

Income from Griffin activities covers less than 40% of our operating costs—leaving an ever-increasing gap for us to fill through government funding, sponsorship and the generosity of our individual supporters. Your support helps us bridge the gap and keep ticket prices affordable and our work at its best. To make a donation and a difference, contact Griffin on **9332 1052** or donate online at **griffintheatre.com.au**

PROGRAM PATRONS

Griffin Ambassadors
Robertson Foundation

Griffin Amplify
Girgensohn Foundation

Griffin Literary Manager
Robertson Foundation

Griffin Studio
Gil Appleton
Darin Cooper Foundation
Kiong Lee & Richard Funston
Ken & Lilian Horler
Malcolm Robertson Foundation
Geoff & Wendy Simpson OAM
Danielle Smith & Sean Carmody

Griffin Studio Workshop
Mary Ann Rolfe (Patron)
Iolanda Capodanno & Juergen Krufczyk
Darin Cooper Foundation
Bob & Chris Ernst
Susan MacKinnon
Pip Rath & Wayne Lonergan
Walking up the Hill Foundation

Griffin Women's Initiative
Katrina Barter
Wendy Blacklock
Jessica Block
Christy Boyce & Madeleine Beaumont
Julieanne Campbell
Iolanda Capodanno
Laura Crennan
Jennifer Darin
Lyndell Droga
Mandy Foley
Judith Fox & Yvonne Stewart
Melinda Graham
Sherry Gregory
Rosemary Hannah & Lynette Preston
Antonia Haralambis
Ann Johnson
Roanne Knox
Tessa Leong
Tory Loudon
Susan MacKinnon
Julia Pincus
Ruth Ritchie
Lenore Robertson
Deanne Weir
Simone Whetton

PRODUCTION PARTNERS 2023

***Jailbaby* by Suzie Miller**
Darin Cooper Foundation
Richard McHugh & Kate Morgan
Bruce Meagher & Greg Waters
Julia Pincus & Ian Learmonth
Andrew Post & Sue Quill

PRODUCTION PARTNERS 2022

***Whitefella Yella Tree* by Dylan Van Den Berg**
Lisa Barker & Don Russell
Darin Cooper Foundation
Robert Dick & Erin Shiel
Lyndell & Daniel Droga
Danny Gilbert AM & Kathleen Gilbert
Rosemary Hannah & Lynette Preston
Bruce Meagher & Greg Waters
Richard McHugh & Kate Morgan
Julia Pincus & Ian Learmonth
Pip Rath & Wayne Lonergan

SEASON DONORS

Company Patron $100,000+
Neilson Foundation

Season Patron $50,000+
Girgensohn Foundation
Robertson Foundation

Mainstage Donors $20,000+
Anonymous (1)
Darin Cooper Foundation
Robert Dick & Erin Shiel
Rosemary Hannah & Lynette Preston
Julia Pincus & Ian Learmonth
Mary Ann Rolfe

Production Donors $10,000+
Lisa Barker & Don Russell
Gordon & Marie Esden
Abraham & Helen James
Ingrid Kaiser
Nathan Mayfield
Richard McHugh & Kate Morgan
Bruce Meagher & Greg Waters
Tim Minchin
Peter & Dianne O'Connell
Pip Rath & Wayne Lonergan
The WeirAnderson Foundation

Rehearsal Donors $5,000–$9,999
Anonymous (1)
Antoinette Albert
Gil Appleton
Wendy Blacklock
Ellen Borda
Bernard Coles
Ian Dickson
Lyndell & Daniel Droga
Danny Gilbert AM & Kathleen Gilbert
Libby Higgin
Ken & Lilian Horler
Lambert Bridge Foundation
Kiong Lee & Richard Funston
Lee Lewis & Brett Boardman

Rosemary Lucas & Robert Yuen
Sophie McCarthy & Antony Green
Catriona Morgan-Hunn
Anthony Paull
Rebel Penfold-Russell OAM
Geoff & Wendy Simpson OAM
The Sky Foundation
Merilyn Sleigh & Raoul de Ferranti
Danielle Smith & Sean Carmody
Walking Up the Hill Foundation

Final Draft Donors
$3,000–$4,999

Corinne & Bryan
Bob & Chris Ernst
Jocelyn Goyen
Sherry Gregory
James Hartwright & Kerrin D'Arcy
Roanne & John Knox
Susan MacKinnon
Don & Leslie Parsonage
Leslie Stern

Workshop Donors
$1,000–$2,999

Anonymous (6)
Melissa Ball
Baly Douglass Foundation
Katrina Barter
Helen Bauer & Helen Lynch AM
Cherry & Peter Best
Jessica Block
Christy Boyce & Madeleine Beaumont
Dr Bernadette Brennan
Anne Britton
Stephen & Annabelle Burley
Iolanda Capodano & Juergen Krufczyk
Julieanne Campbell
Louise Christie
Anna Cleary
Bryony & Tim Cox
Sally Crawford
Laura Crennan
Cris Croker & David West
Ros & Paul Espie
Brian Everingham
Jan Ewert
John & Libby Fairfax
Mandy Foley
Sandra Forbes
Jennifer Giles
Nicky Gluyas
Melinda Graham
Peter Gray & Helen Thwaites
Antonia Haralambis
Kate Harrison
John Head
Mark Hopkinson & Michelle Opie
Michael Jackson
Ann Johnson
David & Adrienne Kitching
Elizabeth Laverty
Benjamin Law
Tessa Leong
Richard & Elizabeth Longes
Tory Loudon
Kyrsty Macdonald & Christopher Hazell
Prudence Manrique
Lorin Muhlmann
Ian Neuss & Penny Young
David Nguyen
Shaan Perera
Ian Phipps
Martin Portus
Annabel Ritchie
In memory of Katherine Robertson
Sylvia Rosenblum
Jann Skinner
Ann & Quinn Sloan
Geoffrey Starr
Stuart Thomas
Elizabeth Thompson
Mike Thompson
Sue Thomson
Janet Wahlquist
Richard Weinstein & Richard Benedict
Simone Whetton
Rob White & Lisa Hamilton
Rosemary White
Paul & Jennifer Winch
Elizabeth Wing

Reading Donors
$500–$999

Anonymous (3)
Brian Abel
Priscilla Adey
Jane Albert
Amity Alexander
Wendy Ashton
Robyn Ayres
Phillip Black
Claire Bornhoffen
Larry Boyd & Barbara Caine AM
Tim Capelin
Jane Christensen
Michael Diamond AM MBE
Max Dingle OAM
Elizabeth Diprose
David Earp
Leonie Flannery
Alan Froude & David Round
Peter Graves
Erica Gray
Stephanie & Andrew Harrison
David Hoskins & Paul McKnight
Sylvia Hrovatin
Nicki Jam
Mira Joksovic
Matt Jones & Rebecca Bourne Jones
Colleen Mary Kane
Susan J Kath
Patricia Lynch
Ian & Elizabeth MacDonald
Suzanne & Anthony Maple-Brown
Robert Marks
Nick Read
Chris Marrable & Kate Richardson
Simon Marrable & Anna Kasper
Christopher Matthies
Christopher McCabe
John McCallum & Jenny Nicholls
Daniela McMurdo
Jacqui Mercer
John Mitchell
Neville Mitchell
Keith Moynihan
Patricia Novikoff
Carolyn Penfold
Belinda Piggott & David Ojerholm
Virginia Pursell
Alex-Oonagh Redmond
Bill Harris
Gemma Rygate
Rob & Rae Spence
Mary Stollery & Eric Dole
Catherine Sullivan & Alexandra Bowen
Ariadne Vromen
Robyn Fortescue & Rosie Wagstaff
Helen Wicker

First Draft Donors
$200-$499

Anonymous (11)
Susan Ambler
Elizabeth Antonievich
William Armitage
Chris Baker
Jan Barr
John Bell AO, OBE

Edwina Birch
Andrew Bowmer
Peter Brown
Wendy Buswell
Ruth Campbell
David Caulfield
Amanda Clark
Sue Clark
Louise Costanzo
Brendan Crotty &
Darryl Toohey
Bryan Cutler
Sue Donnelly
Peter Duerden
Anna Duggan
Kathy Esson
Elizabeth Evatt
Michael Eyers
Helen Ford
Judith Fox
Eva Gerber
Jock Given
Deane Golding
Keith Gow
Virginia & Kieran Greene
Jo Grisard
Edwina Guinness
Ruth Guss
Kate Haddock
Raewyn Harlock

Robert Henderson &
Marijke Conrade
Grania Hickley
Matthew Huxtable
Marian & Nabeel Ibrahim
Andrew Inglis
James Landon-Smith
Penelope Latey
Liz Locke
Danielle Long
Norman Long
Noella Lopez
Maruschka Loupis
Anni MacDougall
Claire McCaughan
Louise McDonald
Duncan McKay
Paula McLean
Stephen McNamara
Anne Miehs
Julia Mitchell
Mark Mitchell
Sarah Mort
Margaret Murphy
Carolyn Newman
Suzanne Osmond
Catherine &
Joshua Palmer
Peter Pezzutti
Christopher Powell
Janelle Prescott

Andrew Pringle
Dorothy & Adit Rao
Tracey Robson
Ann Rocca
Catherine Rothery
Kevin & Shirley Ryan
Dimity Scales
Julia Selby
Natalie Shea
Vivienne Skinner
Bridget Smith
Vanda & Martin Smith
Yvonne Stewart
Augusta Supple
Danny Tomic
Rachel Trigg
Samantha Turley
Adam Van Rooijen
Julie Whitfield
Eve Wynhausen
Robert Yuen
William Zappa

We would also like to thank Peter O'Connell for his expertise, guidance and time.

CURRENT AS OF 10 APRIL 2023

Griffin would like to thank the following:

OUR PARTNERS

Government Supporters

Benefactor

Creative Partners

alphabet.

Company Sponsors

Griffin Theatre Company is assisted by the Australian Government through the Australia Council, its arts funding and advisory body; and the NSW Government through Create NSW.